MICHAEL BENTUM

# MARKED FOR DARKNESS, DESTINED FOR LIGHT

*His own blood held him captive. Jesus' blood would set him free. A true story of God's love in the heart of West Africa.*

D1603025

First published by Michael Bentum  2022

Unless otherwise indicated, all Scripture quotations are taken from the New King James Version, Copyright ©

First edition

ISBN: 9780578384627

Editing by Bobbi Bentum

This book was professionally typeset on Reedsy.
Find out more at reedsy.com

# Contents

# INTRODUCTION

In life there are many seasons. Some are similar the world over, others come to each of us as vastly different as the patterns in snowflakes. I had no idea as a young child all the different seasons my life would pass through; the constraints and freedoms, losses and gains. No matter the season one thing always remained, God was faithful and to this day He is always there for me. God loves every person equally. Because of this I know that His faithfulness over your life is just as sure as it has been over mine.

Yes, seasons change but Jesus is the One who has promised to never leave us nor forsake us. He is the same yesterday, today and forever. As the seasons of this life come and go they come accompanied by the richest joys and at times the most painful pathways. I would like to encourage you that our heavenly Father's goodness and loving watch care for us is unfailing in every season of our lives. Life is unpredictable, but with God life will never be traveled alone, the pain and trials we are sure to face will not be wasted, the evidence of His loving hand will be seen in our journey and the ending will be eternally glorious.

It is my sincerest desire and prayer that in reading about some of the early seasons of my journey, you will be able to see even the smallest glimpse of a most loving God. As you read about the incredible way Jesus pervaded the very tapestry of my own dark childhood I hope your heart is warmed by His supernatural love, compassion and intervention. As you read further about His guidance, grace and encouragement in some of the strangest of days, may you also be inspired to know that no matter what, God is ready to hold your hand in every moment you pass through.

We each have a story, and above all I pray that you will be uplifted as you read my story to stop and retrace the goodness of God in your own life. It matters not whether you have known Him for a lifetime or perhaps are just beginning to feel the gentle pulling of His love for you. The One and only God who is Love Himself sees you right now and His goodness is over you. May the following pages instill the reality that He cares for each of us deeper than any of us will ever fully know.

Michael Bentum

# FORWARD

Though we were only privileged to have our friend Michael Bentum with us in Mozambique for a short time, I could not be more proud of the work he has gone on to do around the world. It has been a real pleasure to learn more of his life and testimony, which contains so many themes to which we can relate! I know what it is like to feel snatched up by God by His choice alone, completely apart from anything I could ever have asked for or imagined. I am forever grateful that God sent me to Africa, but people like Michael are its born treasures and the joys of our work.

Like everyone who perseveres in the gospel, Michael has had to pay a real price for his faith and labors. The challenges he has faced are a genuine darkness in our part of the world — poverty, violence, racism, witchcraft, and more. But as we walk together toward the heavenly kingdom that is coming soon, I believe each trial he has overcome can offer courage and understanding to everyone with an ear to hear.

I pray that everyone who reads this book will find all these things, and be refreshed in hope, faith, and the love from God that is daily gathering His family together from every corner of the world.

Heidi G. Baker, Ph.D.
Co-founder and Executive Chairman of the Board, Iris Global

# Chapter 1 - Dark Etchings

"You saw me before I was born.
Every day of my life was recorded in your book.
Every moment was laid out before a single day had passed.
How precious are your thoughts about me, O God."
~ Psalm 139:16-17 NLT ~

"How does one escape such an inescapable fate? Who in all the universe can protect our baby?"

These were the questions both my parents asked. They struggled to know what to do regarding the soon arrival of another child into their growing family. As the delivery day drew near my Mama, Akuah, knew time was running out for unanswered questions such as these. She looked intently across the dim, one-room hut to where her husband Paul sat, watching him closely to see any glimmer of an answer on his face. If he did have an answer it was somewhere hidden, deep behind his silent eyes.

My sisters Essi and Abba sat together on the dusty floor quite oblivious to our parents pondering. Any understanding as to where their three younger siblings had disappeared to wasn't even a thought in their growing minds. For them, the days slipped by with simple things like food, games, rest and rivalries. Life at such a young age certainly didn't come with the capacity to grasp the strange darkness which hovered overhead and mysteriously lingered around the house.

Even with his troubled spirit Papa's smile remained, he loved his daughters and nothing could take that from him. But how his heart ached for the three children he had so recently buried. It was sudden the way they had gone, far too tragic a loss. These had not been accidents. The three children's deaths were altogether intentional and wrong; harrowing details forever etched as tormenting memories in his mind. The evil intentions behind these malicious attacks would remain unknown. Their deaths came as suddenly and starkly as the darkness that now continuously invaded his home. Beyond a mere disaster of life, the occurrences had been something far more strange and sinister.

What had caused this? Witchcraft - a word, older than the countless generations that came before, still sends shivers of fear up many spines. However, regardless of the fear it caused, witchcraft was simply one of those dreaded but clung to realms of life in Dakojum, our West African village. It was a realm that certainly had no intention of shifting someplace else anytime soon.

Was it someone's jealousy, hatred, or simply a misunderstanding that had caused the children's deaths? There was no telling what justified the curses that had been placed on the Bentum's household. Almost from the day that my parents relocated from Cape Coast to Dakojum, they had enjoyed an honor and relative respect from all.

My father Paul was a humble man and quickly became a sought after elder in the village. Not only this but he was one of the most successful sugar cane farmers in the area, and a gifted mechanic finding joy in pouring some of his profit into the village. Mama was short in height, especially when standing alongside my tall father. However, she stood tall in her own industrious way as a kenkey cook. The steaming sour balls of tasty cooked cornmeal were wrapped in sturdy banana leaves for transport and hailed as a favorite kenkey in the market.

Who could do such a terrible thing to this family? That remained the unanswered question that no one dared to ask. Whoever it was remained silent and not another soul was willing to step forward and admit to knowing anything about the assignment.

The amount of secrecy a small village could hold from one of its own was shocking but quite explainable, the spirit of fear reigned and was found on every side. To the one who showed sympathy, that individual easily could become the next target. But to the one who showed hostility, well, they could easily find themselves facing curses of their own. Yes it was harsh, but that was simply the way it was and no one knew how to escape. Constantly it seemed one man fought against another always using the same old witchcraft as their secret weapon of choice. Little knowing that the very demonic spirits they used were intent on everyone's downfall. What a mess it was.

As for the witchdoctor, his twisted smile remained a constant, you could never quite tell what it meant. From his demonic standpoint he seemed quite untouched from the craziness around. He was, as they say, a very big fish in a small pond. So long as the other witch doctors stayed away from our village, he had most of the say and influence. There were no rivals, there was no opposition. With not a lot to lose and much to gain financially he was generally amiable to all who set foot in his door wanting to do 'business'. Business was good, always good for him. The more problems meant increased opportunity to make a fortune off of the unfortunate. Disaster, unrest, villagers merely seeking revenge, to name a few, were all invitations to engage and practice his craft, always for a fee of course. So no, there wasn't much anyone could do other than to try to move on with life as much as possible, as if nothing had happened in the Bentum home. In many minds, the sooner uneasiness eased back into fearful normalcy the better off everyone would be.

Without giving even a second thought to all the drama surrounding my family, I made my grand arrival at home on a Friday morning. It was September 6, 1979, I was born a healthy, hearty and ready to thrive baby boy.

In my country of Ghana, West Africa, the day of the week on which one is born is significant. Each day of the week has two names attached to it, a boy's name and a girl's name. These names are often chosen for the child. My parents decided to call me Kofi, the common name for boys born on Friday.

A baby is a blessing. And while the dark events of previous months may have been silently whispered among the few, my arrival was cause for celebration. As soon as word was out they came. All the mamas and aunties in the village crowded themselves in and out of our cramped one room hut. They were like fat and happy sardines on the wiggle. Flowing in, with eyes as big as seeing the miracle of new life ever gets, and leaving slowly with smiles from ear to ear. Mama and Papa kept a watchful eye on things as I went from one cuddle to another. Their pride over the successful delivery of their firstborn son mixed together with worry regarding my ongoing safety in those early hours and days.

A short time after my birth my parents settled on what to do regarding the safety of my life. Together they made their way to the only 'help' they knew of. Their hope was of course that the witchdoctor from their previous home in Cape Coast could be paid enough money to protect me from whatever curses and deadly traps were coming from the unseen spirit world. The visit however turned out to be the strangest my parents would ever recall.

Truth being told, the witchdoctor himself would have to admit that it was the strangest visit he had ever had as well. He had been so clearly unprepared, yet obviously compelled, to say what he did. Those words though, where on earth, or beyond, did they come from? They were so out of character it was altogether too incredible to take in. Nonetheless it had all happened as if the Presence of One so much greater was right there hovering over every moment.

Tribal markings on the face of an individual are not uncommon throughout many African countries. However, the planned cutting of my face was not going to be one of these small and common tribal markings. Instead, this type

7

of cutting was to be a specific and intentional way of collecting my blood to be given to the demons. The ceremony would forever mark me physically and seal my life to the spirit world's dark purposes and control, all in exchange for my so-called protection.

Instead of going ahead with his intentions the old witchdoctor had looked up after gazing long at the baby in front of him. Shaking his head to one side, as if to cast from it some unwanted guest, he turned and directed his focus towards my father and stated: "I will not, no, I cannot cut your son. He will be safe from harm, for there's something Great over this boy. I cannot use my knife on him today! No, I will not. Take the baby away."

Once back home, Papa held me close, carefully studying the face of his first living son. What had happened? Closing his eyes he pondered the strangeness of it all. To think how the witchdoctor had not even so much as sharpened his knife. My father's heart filled with gratitude to that unknown Great One. Almost simultaneously to the gratitude in his heart came such an unexplained comfort it sent ripples of happiness across his face. He smiled. Certainly his son was destined for greatness and strength. Papa was determined at this moment to help me become the best of the best. Of course to him, this meant that I would be sent to work alongside the local witchdoctor and learn how to become one - I would then be recognized as a prominent figure in our area gradually gaining my own power and esteem in the spirit world. A sigh of relief could be heard as Papa relaxed in the knowledge that his first son Kofi Bentum would be safe.

Unlike my father, Mama still had serious misgivings about my safety. To her thinking, there had been intense demonic attacks on the family already. One just couldn't be safe enough. No matter what had been said, 'extra protection' was critical and she had the means to acquire it.

Mama, assuming she knew best, went ahead with her plan. The very first chance she found, without informing Papa, she wrapped me in a capulana tightly against her back and started a secret journey to visit her father. Though it made no sense that the 'protection' she sought was to be bought from the very evil spirits who themselves were only intent on destroying, she was determined to carry out her plan.

My grandfather was an aging and very foreboding witchdoctor in a distant village. He was well known for his cunning in witchcraft and to this extent had built his own pagan 'spiritual church'. Dangerous is what many called my mother's entire family. With seemingly no sympathy at all he took me, his own grandson, and slashed not one but twelve gaping wounds to my face. The cuts surrounded my eyes and mouth. It is hard to comprehend, let alone imagine the pain and horror this trauma most certainly caused. The horrific ordeal mercifully has vanished from my memory. An infant at this time, I have no recollection of what took place that day except for the lifelong scars which still are etched across my face.

Blood poured out freely from the gashes. Grandpa carefully collected my pooling blood for his idols and the minion of other evil spirits who required the token. It was a costly and physically irreversible price those demons demanded. Handed over to them for my own safety no less, it was an act that almost cost me my life at the time.

In the days that followed my mother was worried that I would die, even as she did her best to dress the knife marks with a topical potion her father had given her to use. Considering I was cut down to the facial bones, with no sterile procedures taken, no follow up stitching or sanitary after care given, it was a miracle I survived the ordeal.

What darkness covered our land and people. Not only was human blood required for my life insurance, but by this very act I was in that darkest moment dedicated to the demonic world. A blood covenant linking my life to all that is death.

This ordeal must have been on many levels traumatic for my mother to witness. However, this was the choice Mama made that day from her own place of blind darkness. The cruel and brutal ways of witchcraft were not unfamiliar to her, as she herself had been entrenched her entire life in this culture. It hadn't been Papa's decision for me to be marked so traumatically but now that the ritual had been carried out, he agreed with Mama that it was the best decision. He knew his son had a future of importance and was now thoroughly connected to a destiny of idol worship. In his mind, to have me dedicated in such a dramatic way was in fact confirmation of a prestigious future. In many ways my parents' prior worry was soon replaced with pride and a sense of security as to what my future held. While intended as the very chain linking me to the grip of darkness, my scars have become a constant visual reminder to me of the redeeming power of Jesus.

# Chapter 2 - Dokojum Days

**"But God showed His love to us.**
**While we were still sinners, Christ died for us."**
**~ Romans 5:8 NLV ~**

I grew up in Ghana, in a typical African village surrounded by a culture that was far removed from western influence. Many changes have come to Ghana since the years when I was a small boy, however, regardless of how many things have changed in Africa, or in our world as a whole, the lessons I learned growing up were much the same as most parents seek to instill in their children the globe over.

I was not raised in a christian home, my house was a place where idol worship was as common as the hair on our heads. Our family worshiped demons, ate with idols and honored our ancestors. A simple hole in the dirt right outside our door held a bottle of alcohol and was set there as an altar connecting to my father's altar inside the house. One whole corner of our small one room home was dedicated to the inside altar and contained tokens that connected it with yet another altar in Cape Coast. In addition to the pagan rituals of daily life, we also celebrated village wide pagan festivities throughout the year. It is hardly a surprise that growing up I never heard the words of scripture, "Honor your father and your mother." This sentence was not even a thought in my brain, however, the timeless value of this virtue remains important no matter who you are, what you've read, or where you live. To the best of their ability,

Papa and Mama sought to teach us the importance of respecting our elders and leading an honest life.

While my family was certainly not the poorest in the village, it still took everyone of us doing our part in order to make ends meet. As soon as our feet stood us up straight, my siblings and I began learning how to work. One of my first memories is learning to carry a bucket on my head. This skill is part of what makes an African out of a boy or girl. Training must start from the moment our baby eyes can focus on mama's head piled high above us as we go about the day strapped securely to her back in a capulana cloth. Gradually as we grow we imitate, play and learn. Small empty buckets topple off but eventually become large filled ones that stay in place. A sturdy spot to carry things on one's head comes in quite useful on numerous occasions. Quickly the little skills that were taught in the house enabled my siblings and I to take on bigger jobs further from home.

On the weekends, early in the morning I would go with Papa to our family farm. My task was to take my machete using it to cut sugar cane on the farm and tend the water yams. Once collected I would sell the cane and yams by stacking them in piles on the street. This provided me with money to go to school. The sugary wood from the cane was like snack food and hungry people bought it quickly. It didn't cost a lot, two cedi and one cedi bunches equaling about twenty to thirty American cents. To make a bit more money and to pass the time while waiting for my sugar cane to sell I would carefully chop and then peel some of the canes, transforming the gnarly branches into ready-to-eat and glistening white tender sticks. Instead of plastic bags, which could not be found and therefore were not used in our village, I wrapped the prepared cane with our readily available banana leaves. These sweet treats sold for a small amount more and saved the hungry buyer the hassle of peeling their own.

**Crab Hunting**

While I enjoyed my farming responsibilities, there was absolutely nothing surpassing the spine-tingling excitement that came from hunting field crabs. The thought of tender crab meat was prize enough for the risky business of trying to catch the critters. Crab hunting at best was a treacherous task and therefore all of us village boys bravely took it on as our own manly responsibility. We'd wait until the heat of the day when our courage had time to soar and the crabs were soaking themselves out in the sunshine, they were easiest to spot at this time of day. Once our sights were fixed we would sneak up on the unsuspecting crabs with steady fingers and pounding hearts. Of course, as soon as they saw us coming they'd run as only a crab evading capture can. Quick as a flash they'd be scuttling down their damp dark holes to prepare for war, and this was where the real men were separated from the boys. Here at the juncture of ground level and den wall came our crucial moment of reckoning. If we could catch the crab before it reached the end of the burrow, we'd be safe. If not, we'd be met with a crab on defense whose large pincers were ready to grab onto our intruding fingers with a vengeance not quickly forgotten. The holes were about an arms-length in depth and the crabs were about the size of a squashed potato. It was a daring escapade to say the least and not one for the fearful. I cannot recall anything else in childhood that felt quite so victorious as pulling a crab from one of those holes. Crab soup was the best, especially when served with a side of water yams. The whole family was delighted for this rare treat, which only happened when fear was exchanged for the valiant duties of a successful crab hunt.

**A soapy lesson learned**

I was not always so devoted to providing good experiences for our family. As a young boy of seven I had much to learn about obedience. One sweltering day a memorable lesson was headed my way. Papa's parting request, "please wash my clothes", as he left for the farm one morning was not what I was wanting to hear. Especially when the other ear was listening to my good friend Charles calling for me from outside to come play soccer. Soccer sounded so much more enticing than washing stinky soiled clothes. With a grumble I waited until Papa was out of sight and then scooped up all the clothes and tossed them in a bucket with water and soap. It was a good half job and that was good enough for me. *I'll get back to it after the game,* I promised myself. Dashing out the door I hurried to catch up with my friends. My bare feet kicked up the dust on the trail as I joined the others, it was going to be a great day.

Our one game led to two games and before I realized it the day had passed. The setting sun began casting long shadows across the landscape just about the same time that my tired body began reminding me how very hungry it was. I came home late and saw Papa already home from the farm and sitting by the front door. He waited until I was close before asking if I had finished washing the clothes. The clothes! They were still wet and dirty where I had left them that morning. I did not answer him, instead I ran away. I knew I was in for a beating, so I ran fast only daring to creep inside late in the night once everyone was sleeping. Being all of one tiny room, there weren't many places to hide in our mud brick house so I hid under my parents' bed on the cold dirt floor. To my seven year old thinking, under the bed certainly was the most secret place where surely nobody would think to look.

In my hurry the day before I had put Papa's clothes in the very same bucket he used for baths. The next morning he found the bucket and the clothes at the back of the house. It wasn't until he reached under the bed to collect his sandals that he found me. He pulled me out from under the bed by one foot. I couldn't run away this time. As I was bracing for the strike of his hand Papa said he would not beat me but instead he told me someone would do this same thing to me and I would learn what it felt like.

A few days later my little sister Sarah, who loved to wash our clothes, gathered all the washing together. For reasons I never could understand, it didn't seem to matter to Sarah whose clothes they were, she would always scavenge around for every last one. I suppose she found the bubbles and froth of washing fun. Chances are my father had asked her to teach me a lesson; or maybe not. Whatever the case happened to be, the lesson was learned. On this particular day she washed everything except for my school uniform which she left soaking in a big pan of soapy water.

Now I need to mention that my school uniform was very important to me. You see, it was the only normal and nice piece of clothing I owned. All the other days at home and working on the farm I wore an oversized and tattered shirt. The shirt served as my trousers, underwear and shirt all in one messy array of distressed cloth. It wasn't new and didn't provide the support that a nice pair of trousers would have given, but it was all I had, other than my decent school uniform that is.

On Monday I went looking for my uniform to wear to school. After searching all over I finally found it all soapy and wet, still soaking in Sarah's wash water. I desperately didn't want to go to school and Papa was sure to remind me of the lesson I had coming. What I learned that day has stayed with me. Do to others as you would have them do to you. I found the golden rule for the first time right within those soapy suds.

**Steps of pain and safety**

'I'm going to take a shortcut right here,' I decided one afternoon on my way home from school. It was a shortcut through a junkyard. This place was full of discarded items and rusting appliances. The stench from rotting garbage and the occasional pig rooting through the trash usually was enough to warrant the longer bypass to home. However, on this particular day I decided to take my chances and cut through. I almost made it, but not quite. As I was leaving the place my foot landed squarely on an old rusted nail. It dug deep into the flesh of the sole of my foot. My siblings and I hardly ever wore shoes. Sometimes we acquired sandals made from the tread of old car tires, but mostly we couldn't be bothered fussing with shoes. My feet were very tough from daily barefoot use, but they were not tough enough to handle nails. Somehow I made it home. Scarcely able to walk I was left with no doubt that I had made a very poor choice.

Papa was quick to come to my rescue. I was glad at first but still recall his cure for my throbbing foot was almost worse than the initial nail going in. He knew the danger of rust and poisons that could cause a nasty infection. To sanitize and clean my wounded foot, he used Shea butter. Shea butter is grown a lot in the north of Ghana and has a multitude of uses. Taking the Shea butter Papa heated it to a melting point over the fire and then poured the oil over the open nail hole on my foot. In spite of the brutal treatment, in time it completely healed over, with no infection.

Sadly, this injury did not teach me about staying on the path. For some funny reason I liked walking home from school in random places. One day Sarah and I were on our way home from the schoolhouse. For whatever our childish reasons were for avoiding the road, we chose instead to walk in the gutter. I wasn't looking at my feet as I walked along. All of a sudden I couldn't put my foot down when I went to take a step. *'That's odd'* I thought to myself. I attempted once more, but still my foot would not go down. I glanced at the ground right in front of me and there, right under the place my foot would have landed, lay a large deadly snake. One strike from this snake and I would have been dead within minutes. Sarah stood right behind me and both of us were frozen in panic, all I could do was yell for help as two men were passing on the road above. They quickly jumped to our rescue and killed the snake. Upon seeing the snake lifeless and still, no longer able to do us harm, our fearfully frozen muscles began to thaw. To say we felt relief would be quite the understatement. Sarah and I launched ourselves faster than a flash back up onto the main road and went straight home. Later that night my father nodded solemnly when I told him about the near accident with the deadly snake. "Son, there is a huge battle over your life. You have a great destiny to fulfill as a witch doctor one day." he said.

# Chapter 3 - In Search Of Power

**"I have even called you by your name... though you have not known Me.**
**I am the Lord, and there is no other;**
**There is no God besides Me."**
**~ Isaiah 45 ~**

"Sarah, time to get up!" I nudged my younger sister awake. My older sisters no longer went to school so it was just Sarah and I. Every school day was almost the same for us. Just before daybreak we woke up to take our baths and be on our way. Papa, who never had the opportunity to go to school, often sent us out the door with the parting words, "I'm so happy you have this chance!" The school we went to was a two and a half hour walk from our village. We didn't mind the distance, and hardly even thought about how far it was. School was where our friends were and in those days we walked everywhere.

It wasn't long before we were ready and out of the house on our way to school. Soon the dusty village streets gave way to a narrow dirt pathway that went back and forth through the bush like a slithering snake. Lining this path stood the tall African grasses so thick we could not see through. They reached high above us waving their heads in the morning breeze.

Often on the walk to school we could catch glimpses of fat little animals as they darted in and out of the grass. Early morning was the best time to see these critters. Soon they would be disappearing deeper into the bush to escape the intense midday heat. There were many varieties of small animals but we called them all by just one name, bushmeat. They came from the bush and they were edible, but not always catchable. More often than not we would just point them out and watch as they scampered away.

"Let's cut through the cemetery." Sarah suggested. "Good idea, let's do this," I heartily agreed. Often we chose this route as it gave us a small shortcut to class. We turned off the regular track and made our way to the dismal plot of land full of graves. I always found it hard to imagine all the people lying beneath our feet. It was a lot easier, and certainly nicer, to think about what was above the ground, like the old sour orange tree growing in the cemetery.

For as long as I could remember this orange tree had stood there like a solitary sentinel, dressed in a ridiculous orange dotted uniform, rigidly guarding the cemetery. We loved this tree as it always seemed to be fully loaded with fruit. We loved it even more on the days when lunch money was not available. We could always count on going to the cemetery, sitting on a gravestone and filling our stomachs with oranges. The oranges were very sour ones but fortunately for us, there was another tree close by that grew an incredible seed. This seed was sweet like sugar and if eaten along with the orange made the sour slices sweet. Nibbles of seed and bites of orange made for a great lunch.

I was still thinking about oranges when the long narrow school building came into view. The shutters were open and huddles of students stood idly around. "Teacher is not here today," a fellow student yelled as we walked closer. This did not surprise me at all, it seemed that the teacher not being at school was far more common than her being there. For some reason our school had a hard time keeping teachers. Sometimes the teacher just wouldn't show up for a whole week. We didn't worry too much because in our minds no teacher merely meant lots more soccer.

My friends and I spent our time chasing a soccer ball around the field. The girls, well, I don't know what they did but whatever it was they also passed the day somehow. When the shadows began to lengthen we said goodbye to our friends and headed back to the path that would eventually lead us home before nightfall.

## "Where are we going?"

It had been a good day and dusk was quickly approaching. Just beyond the village I watched as the sun sunk below the bush, snuggling in as if for another night under a faithful blanket of darkness. Around the corner of the house my older sister Essi hurried and came in. Her hands were filled with a bundle of green banana leaves. Sitting next to Mama by the fire they each took a leaf and proceeded to hold it over the hot smoke rising from the smoldering embers. In no time at all the fresh and fibrous leaves were wilted, faded and as floppy as fluffy blankets, minus the fluff. My siblings and I gladly took the warm leaves handed to us and wrapped them around ourselves as best as we could. Now we also could snuggle into the dark night, warm and dry. We didn't use banana leaves every night, but when the air became chilly they made a big difference.

As I drifted off to sleep the last thing on my mind was how very differently the next day would turn out. What a surprise when I was woken late that night and told by Papa we were going far away on a 'special journey.' I'm not sure the reason but Papa always traveled at night. Rolling out of bed I pulled on my school uniform as fast as I could. Before even the village rooster had time to wake up, we were well on our way. The night air was crisp and cool as I hurried to keep up with Papa's long strides. "Where are we going?" I wondered aloud. Papa smiled down at me but right behind his smile I couldn't help noticing a hint of seriousness. "You'll know soon enough." He replied. I was curious and excited. A surprise? I liked surprises.

After walking for what seemed a very long time, we entered the city of Kumasi. Cars and trucks, animals and people were going every direction. I held tightly to Papa's hand as we maneuvered our way through the crowded streets. "I don't think this city ever stops," Papa laughed as he pushed me past a drowsy looking policeman. I had never been to the city in my life. There was so much activity happening all at once. This certainly made our market day in the village seem like nothing. "Is this my surprise?" I asked Papa in awe, with eyes wide open, I did not want to miss a single thing around me. "Oh no, not yet." Papa replied.

## Locating the locomotive

All at once out of nowhere a loud whistle erupted. Sailing out into the air it soared with such authority everyone had to pay attention. "What was that?" I gasped. It was louder than every other city noise. In fact, the sound of it caused my mouth to drop open in amazement even as Papa gripped my hand tighter and picked up his pace. My short legs propelled me forward as on we flew. What was going to happen next? We rounded a corner and that is when Papa pointed to the most unusual object I had ever seen. The way people were entering the thing and exiting it, perhaps it was a vehicle, but to me it appeared more like a monstrous machine. Seeing my amazement Papa explained, "That is a train son."

The cars of the train all hooked together, held by hundreds of wheels. It reminded me of a giant centipede. I was fascinated. Who could drive this large train? I thought. Certainly this must be the surprise. But when I asked Papa he still shook his head 'no' and started talking with a man who had come up to us. The man seemed very busy and important as he took the money Papa offered him. In return the man stuffed two strips of paper into Papa's hand. "All Aboard!" someone shouted from the left.

We joined the stream of people and began shuffling all together in one direction. Try as I might, it was hard to see where we were going. I had a suspicion and sure enough, before I knew it, we were boarding the train itself. *How can this not be my surprise?* I wondered. I was very glad that Papa was right there with me. I was excited and nervous to be on the train and to be honest my legs were shaking just a little. Whatever the surprise was, it must be extremely important to warrant a trip to the city and a train ride as well. I sat in the hard seat swinging my shaking legs and watching with excitement as the land outside started to pass our window faster and faster. Soon we had chugged our way out of the station and right out of Kumasi.

We were headed for Takoradi. Upon arriving it didn't take long to realize that Takoradi was another big city, full of all the same interesting sights, sounds and smells I had experienced in Kumasi. Takoradi was just as overwhelming, I don't think I ever let go of Papa's hand the entire journey. It felt very comforting and secure to know that he was right there by my side, I couldn't help wondering how in the world he knew where to go. He was confident that we would not get lost.

**Distressing discovery**

With such a dramatically exciting journey to Takoradi, I was almost disap-pointed to find that our travels ended in a rather ordinary place. The compound we came to rest in was not big, in fact it was stinky and small. Scruffy looking chickens were picking their way through rubbish as the flies buzzed about. I didn't see why we had to come all this way just to sit in a compound like so many back home. Couldn't we have accomplished such a feat right in our own village? But here we were and the only thing left to do was wait. Surely soon now I would find out my surprise.

And then it happened, the door of one of the compound buildings opened and its occupant stepped out. I sucked in my breath and gulped in surprise. One quick look at Papa and I knew that this was the surprise. While what I saw was not foreign to me, it still landed far beyond all the craziness of everything I'd seen up to this point. Forget about curiosity, I didn't want this surprise after all. There before us stood the most hideously dressed witchdoctor beckoning us into his demonic house. All the pieces started to fall into place in my mind as I began to recall the many times Papa had told me that my life would be one

21

of importance. I had heard the stories surrounding my birth and I knew both my parents wanted me to become a witch doctor someday.

I was not totally opposed to their aspirations for my future, but did it have to be today? I didn't want to go, I didn't want to hold Papa's hand anymore. I felt the spirit of fear rising up on my insides as I desperately tried to think of how to escape. I was still vainly grasping for ideas as we entered the room. Papa was holding me tight now, he kept telling me to be brave and to behave. "I'm not brave and I won't behave!" I cried out. Once inside I saw more equally large men, I was totally outnumbered and smaller than them all.

The witchdoctor seemed to know exactly why we were there, as did my father and all the other men. They told me, "It is time for you, son, to receive power!" The witchdoctor's mysterious chanting started filling the room and as if on cue the other men stepped closer. One took my right leg and another took my left. Angry tears punched their way from my eyes as I thrashed violently with my only free hand. All too soon I found this last free hand caught in the grasp of yet another strong grip coming from behind me. I wiggled, squirmed and screamed but I couldn't get away. It wasn't worth even trying, but try I did. Every limb I owned was caught in a grip larger and stronger than my own as these cruel men pinned my small body to the floor.

I keenly recall how my desperate shouting seemed to frustrate the witchdoctor's focus. He had trouble locating the demonic spirits. In looking back at this moment I truly believe the Lord was standing with me even in the midst of this dreadful ordeal. Could it have been that the witchdoctor's frustrated lack of connection to his demons was merely due to my shouting? Or was the Lord once more fighting for my life with a love I had yet to comprehend?

I wanted to close my eyes but found it impossible as the chanting witchdoctor came closer and closer with his sharp knife pointed at me. As the demonic doctor continued his approach, all I could now see was the glistening metal of his sharp but filthy knife blade. *Don't I have enough marks from demons already, aren't you satisfied with my blood?* My mind screamed the question but there was no answer. It was as if I was in the middle of a horrific nightmare, only it wasn't a bad dream I could wake from, I was living it. The terrifying witchdoctor used his knife to cut multiple gashes across my limbs and body. Intentional sets of three with nine sets total. He inscribed with his knife a series of marks on each of my wrists, on each elbow, each shoulder, each side of my ribs and then one right in the middle of my chest. The only anesthetic available to numb the pain was the shock induced by the brutal ordeal. Quickly following this extremely painful ritual he took a potion of black demonic medicine and filled each of the twenty seven gaping wounds. When I was finally released from the death grip they had restrained me with, my school clothes were soaked from a mixture of black potion, perspiration and blood. I was eight years old.

Right there in the dim room all my fear quickly turned to hateful anger. The spirit of anger settled deep into my heart over the following days. Like a dark fog it was filling me up. Once my wounds healed over, giving way to scars which would remain, a lot had changed for me. I never felt a physical difference in my body, all I knew was that nobody could overtake me in a fight. And fight I did. I was shocked the first time I beat up not one, but two village boys at the same time. Both of them were stronger, older and taller than I.

No matter how traumatically and demonically it had all started, I came to the place where I liked the power that I now carried. It was a tangible dark power that I wore with pride among my peers. As time passed I barely noticed the cloud over me. But I did realize the childhood innocence I had once known was now gone. However, I didn't even come close to understanding how incredibly imprisoned I was.

**"God is calling you."**

Stealing a chicken was the first thing on my mind that memorable day. Going to church on the other hand wasn't even the last thing on my mind, it simply wasn't on my mind at all. It was dry season in Ghana, and good weather was practically a daily event. Good weather always made for a market day that was full to overflowing with people and supplies. And many people, loaded with their many supplies, created the prime opportunity to steal chickens. That's right, steal chickens. Getting away with chicken thievery was as easy a task as it took for a small boy to disappear among the bustle of market crowds and activity.

My mind began to anticipate fried chicken as soon as my eyes opened that morning. Without breathing one word of our plans to family I hurried away to meet up with my friends. Together we would catch and eat our fill of chicken. Absorbed in delicious thought I was not prepared or happy to come face to face with Habbakuk. Here was the last person I wanted to meet, the christian evangelist himself. The man, though only having been in our village a short time, had a certain uncanny way of finding me at what I viewed as the worst of times. The worst of times was every time, like today on my way to steal a chicken. I tried to avoid eye contact but it was too late because Habbakuk seemed to have eyes like a lion. He spotted me from a distance and promptly made a beeline my way. Letting out a sigh of frustration I stood as tall as ten years can tower and glared up at him as he loomed above and boomed heartily, "Hello Kofi, just who I have been looking for!" I didn't reply. *How does he know my name?* The puzzling question barely came to mind before an answer quickly followed. *Charles, that rascal, I am sure of it!*

My friend Charles had recently started attending the children's ministry at the christian church in our village. He loved it and was enthralled by what he was learning. Come to think of it, he had actually declined joining us for our chicken chase today. This was the first time he had not joined us for chicken catching in the history of, well, our entire lives. Something strange was happening to Charles and surely he must have been the one who told evangelist Habbakuk my name.

Breaking into my thoughts Habakkuk declared, "God is calling you, God wants

24

to use you! God has a calling on your life." There was such certainty in his voice it made me confused. Inwardly I asked, *Which god? Why me?* My ears were deaf to this strange thing called Christianity.

The very thought of God wanting me was the strangest idea I could imagine. Whoever this God was that Habakkuk talked of, well - as far as I was concerned - that God didn't even know me. And, I for sure, didn't know Him. My momentary daze did not last long: Shaking my head, I shouted my thoughts to the evangelist. "Well, I don't want God!" With those parting words, I spun around and darted down the closest alleyway I could find.

"I'm sorry I'm late, I had to take a detour." I confessed to my friends as I joined them a few minutes later. After a brief huddle we dispersed to our separate 'stations' and the chicken chase was on.

**The last chicken chase**

It wasn't hard to find a chicken as there were plenty of them in the market. All I had to do was wait for one of the boys to stealthily open a cage without being seen and let a chicken go free. Then it was my turn to chase the bird, hopefully in the right direction of course. As it so happened my eyes and stomach were soon intently focused on one hapless chicken. I raced through the marketplace that day as fast as I could. The chicken zipped around stalls, and I raced after it through crowds. We darted past the frowns and jumped over piles of fresh produce. Before anyone could stop our pursuit both the chicken and I roared out of the market and down the path. Leaving the angry shouts far behind we flew from the market, disappearing exactly where we'd planned, straight into the bush.

"Yes, we're doing it again!" James declared as he saw me coming. Another chicken stolen swiftly and successfully, or so my friends and I thought. We prided ourselves, boasting that our plan always pulled off without a hitch. Certainly this was an art only perfected by much practice. I had lost count of how many times, safely hidden in the bush, we had prepared chicken and eaten together, savoring each stolen bite. Little did we know that today would be all-together different.

Within minutes of its valiant run for freedom, poor chicken junior lay roasting over the fire. Amid laughter, savory smells and crackles of soon to be edible food, I thought to myself, *Can life ever become more delightful?*

Well, whether it could or not was a topic that would have to wait for another day. Right at that very moment before any one of us could even jump, our party was crashed by none other than one irate, late chicken owner. The angry man burst upon us with unexpected fury. We were caught chicken-in-hand. This was quickly followed by lashes and lessons, both memorable but neither appreciated. When the man felt satisfied that justice was served he scooped up the remaining meat and left abruptly the way he had come.

I trudged home that evening with pain still smarting from the blows, empty feelings inside and chicken dinner far away on another plate. *Life more delightful?* The question returned only this time it came with an answer that caused my face to scrunch into a frown. *It may or may not get more delightful, but it certainly can get a whole lot worse!* I kicked a rock out of my way and watched as it rolled into a clump of weeds and stuck there. My thoughts that evening were long and sober ones.

It seemed out of nowhere that Charles joined me on the path and I only realized he was there when I heard him repeat, "where have you been? Can you hear me brother?" "Yes, yes I can hear you, what is it?" I replied with a tinge of resentment in my voice. "I was asking if you are coming to the church tonight for the program?" The grin over Charles' face clearly indicated that this was an excellent idea to accept. "I'm not going Charles. Not going! I don't want anything to do with church stuff. If you want to go, fine but leave me out because I hate it." I blurted. To this Charles shrugged his shoulders and sighed, "How do you know you hate it if you've never even been?" I glared at him long enough for him to continue, "Well, suit yourself but you're missing out."

As the two of us parted ways even more confusing thoughts rolled around inside my head. I didn't know what to make of them but one thing I knew, I would never lower myself to Charles level and go to that church. Whatever weird notion had gotten into my friend I was determined it would never catch me.

Needless to say after such a shattering episode of chicken stealing, my friends and I had to seriously rethink our pastimes. Having been caught even this one time, the word was out about who the guilty culprits were. To risk being caught again would be outright disaster. Truthfully speaking there were other quite sensible activities that we had fun with. Even while we didn't have access to commercially made toys, what we could do was construct our own 'limited edition' toy cars to play with. We often scoured our homes and neighborhoods for old milk bottles and tins. By cutting and bending the containers we formed our fancy, far-flung vehicles. To attach all the pieces into a vehicle that held together, we'd use grass reed fibers or if we were in luck, rusty wire bits. Wheels were cut into shape from old sandals or caps from bottles if the car was a small one. Such creative time was spent designing our cars and we had fun playing with the finished products.

The evangelist still found me from time to time and always when he did would share with me how God had a plan for my life, a special destiny for me to fulfill. I never believed a word he said, and in fact, there was only one time I seriously listened to him. I saw him coming towards the front door of our one room hut and so I made a quick departure attempt out the back only to look up and find him waiting there for me with a smile. Habakkuk promised, "If you come to our children's day celebration, you can eat all the food you want and then leave, you don't have to stay for the service." That sounded like a reasonable deal and so I relented and went with him to the church. 'Don't miss the food' was a life principle for me. I ate a good meal and slipped away quite happily before a prayer was prayed or story shared.

# Chapter 4 - Pivotal Changes

"But now in Christ Jesus you who once were far off
have been brought near by the blood of Christ.
For He Himself is our peace -
and has broken down the middle wall of separation."
~ Ephesians 2:13-14 ~

There was much to start anticipating. In less than two weeks the annual festival to the spirits was coming. This was the most highly anticipated feast and yearly observed in appreciation to the spirits who we believed gave us good harvests and safety throughout the previous year. It was a time full of celebration, food, dancing, and sacrifice to idols. I loved this event when everything in sight was so festive, ceremonial and awesomely awful. Perhaps my favorite part was watching the great cooking pots bubbling with stew, or the way that everyone danced. The witchdoctor performed so many sacrifices in recognition of the unseen spirits, it was hard to keep track of them all. I didn't like all the blood and killing, but, these sacrifices made for a lot of food and I liked food.

Yes, I loved food and what better way to enjoy it than eating lots of it when there was plenty to be found on that day. To be honest, there wasn't a lot of food consistently available every day so the yearly feast was a very big deal. In our home we didn't have the modern convenience of a freezer, refrigerator or even a pantry. My siblings and I quickly learned that when food came in abundance you always tried to eat as much of it as possible. My favorite food growing up was the typical Ghanaian dish called banku. Banku is a sticky fermented cornmeal ball usually eaten with soup, or hot pepper and fish. Banku was my favorite food not only because of its distinct and sour flavor, but also because it was a heavy food and one that filled you completely. In fact, it could last you from morning 'til night. After a meal of banku you knew that the day ahead would be one where hungry feelings stayed far away.

As the festival day drew near I couldn't help keeping an eye on the activity that was going on by the big tree. This old tree sat at the corner of our village accompanied only by a small creek which ran behind it. Each year this spot became the central location for many villagers as they prepared for the festival. The tree was used as an altar for pagan rituals and the demonic presence in this particular location was tangible. As for the tree itself it was ancient with limbs that created a wealth of shade as they stretched far and wide. Under the branches of the tree, piles of wood were stacked ready to feed the large fire that would be lit for the festival. Staked here and there were sheep and cows, beside them were small wire cages stacked and filled with noisy chickens and ducks.

Nowhere among all the sacrificial animals could you ever find pigs or goats. The demons always rejected them. I have since learned that in the Bible the wicked are likened to goats, and pigs were never sacrificed to God as they were unclean. Could this be a reason why the demons also rejected them? Whatever the reason, the witchdoctor would never accept an offering of a goat or pig. These animals were considered foul and unwanted by the spirits and they were not eaten in our home either. I only recall one time when I tried to secretly eat some pork; Papa found me before I even had a chance to try it. Immediately the meat was thrown away along with the now deemed useless bowl which had held the forbidden meat.

In addition to the animals, people brought many offerings of fruits and vegetables, grain and local alcohol, baskets and embroidery. Nothing was spared in making this event a display of grandeur. With so many preparations happening, the anticipation was hard to handle as each day closer to the festival brought with it new colors, smells and sights. I could hardly wait, and then right on time the day arrived.

Early in the morning I went with Papa to take a last load of sugar cane to add to the multitude of offerings brought by others. We were glad that it had been a good harvest this year. As soon as we got there I went on the lookout for a good spot to sit, it was hard to find any spot as the place was already filling with people. Papa started talking to one of the men and right about then I smiled because there in front of me was the perfect place. *How has it remained unclaimed?* Piled up against the trunk of the old tree lay a solitary mound of dirt. It was tall enough that by standing on top of the pile I could clearly see what was going on. Running to the tree I staked my spot on the ground. Before long I was engulfed in the full activities of this monumental day.

**A rock to my head**

All at once, and seemingly out of nowhere, a large rock whizzed out of the air and hit squarely and forcefully on the top of my head. Letting out a yell, my hands flew to my head as pain shot through the skin. There on the ground by my feet the rock that hit me was rolling to a stop. Before the rock had time to quit moving I felt a surge of hot anger well up from deep inside me. *Some scoundrel has just struck me with a homemade slingshot,* I concluded. *They're certainly in for it now, I'm going to beat them proper.* I fumed and began scanning the crowd, desperately looking for the guilty culprit. With mounting frustration I saw no one who looked suspicious, not even one slingshot was visible anywhere. My head was starting to throb painfully even as the sea of African faces in front of me began swaying this way and that. Everything around me was becoming blacker than ever before. Dizzily, I stumbled over to Papa and grabbed his shirt desperately, just as much to stay upright as to get his attention.

"Someone hit me with a rock on my head. Papa, I feel horrible!" the words poured out. I didn't want to cry, but already I could feel the start of tears as Papa put a reassuring hand on my shoulder. He helped me sit down on the ground and said, "What you need is some warm soup son, that will help you feel better. You're hungry." I couldn't understand how soup would be a help in a situation like this, nevertheless, Papa's words sounded hopeful so I tried to be hopeful also. I closed my eyes for a minute to stop the world from spinning as Papa went quickly to collect a bowl of sacrifice soup for me. A woman ladled from the boiling pot and dished up a hearty serving of the soup that was cooking over the open fire. How I had dreamed of this meal and yet now as I tried bravely to eat it all I could handle were barely two swallows. A fresh surge of pain shot from the top of my head downwards. The more I ate the soup the worse I began to feel, "I have to go home." I told Papa.

Papa helped me to the hut before returning to the festival. Alone inside, I went straight to bed. I lay down flat on the bed trying to ease my head and forget about the throbbing. Pain radiated from the bump that had raised itself like an obscure egg on top of my head. The tiny dark room was better than the noisy crowd and I gratefully closed my eyes. Almost immediately after closing my eyes a very amazing thing happened - something so incredible, in fact, that it would change the course of the rest of my life.

The next thing I knew was that my spirit was entering the sky. Straight up into the atmosphere I felt myself go. I was dumbfounded as to what was happening but powerless to do anything about it. My body was not doing anything. In fact, as I went upwards I could see my body still lying on the bed inside my tiny house. My thoughts raced, *How can I be up here and my body still be down there, where am I going anyway?* I was totally confused but before I could wonder too much about what was happening to me I came to an incredible place like no other. The One to welcome me into this place introduced Himself as Jesus. *Jesus? Who was Jesus?* I had never heard of Him before and yet there was something so irresistible and compelling about this Man. The warmth of His loving eyes mesmerized me and without a word being spoken I knew I was fully loved and would never be the same. When Jesus told me to follow Him, follow Him I did.

Prior to this day I didn't even know that heaven existed, I had never heard of heaven. But when I met Jesus I instantly knew where I was and that this was heaven. Earthly descriptions quickly run out when trying to explain this place, it is too amazing. The word 'amazing' even is not right! It is a useless word to describe heaven. When in heaven everything from earth becomes very distant, and yet, from earth it is very difficult to explain anything from heaven. All I can say is that heaven was and continues to be the most beautiful place I have ever seen or experienced. Heaven is real! That is what I know!

## Realms of glory, revelation of love

As I have mentioned, words are vastly lacking, but I will do my best to somehow describe what I saw. One of the things I saw while walking with Jesus could only be described as the Glory of God. It was as if it were a fountain flowing and flowing more abundantly. It was so beautiful, alive and vibrant. It was like a visible atmosphere. There were so many other things that I saw and it was hard to comprehend. Everything shone with a radiant splendor.

Jesus then took me out of one place and we were instantly in another. In this place there was a throne. The chair was indescribably wonderful, it was most beautiful but once again, I don't know how to describe this throne. One thing I clearly recall is that Jesus sat down on it and then pointing, said to me, "Look!" When I looked I was shocked at what I saw. Far below me, as if I were perched on a high vantage point looking over a railing, I could clearly see the place where they were doing the sacrifices at home. The pagan festival was now well under way. The killing of chickens, ducks, sheep and cows was happening alongside the dancing and cooking of food for the idols worship. It was organized chaos and very noisy. The fetish priest was cutting his tongue. And like he did every year, he cut it completely off before he demonically attached it again, the blood was everywhere. Many other people were also cutting their bodies and the deep red blood was flowing.

In one regard I was so familiar with the pagan ceremonies and rituals, but now from heaven everything about it was completely wrong. I did not like what I was viewing but it wasn't an option to look away. The atrocity of what I was seeing from this new perspective made me want to cry out for everyone to stop. Jesus came and stood beside me, and His very presence calmed me. He asked me a question that I had never thought of before, and it was a question I will never forget. He asked, "Among all the things that you have been watching has anyone sacrificed themselves for you to be saved? Has anyone given and shed his full blood for you before?" Again I could see all the blood that was flowing from the pagan worship and I knew in that moment like never before that not one single drop of it was selflessly given for me or any other human. I only knew the demons demanded blood and more blood, they never had enough. Someone selflessly giving their own blood was a concept that was new to me. Who would choose to sacrifice themselves in order to save someone else?

We moved to another place. From here as we looked out, all was fire before us. A huge fire, bigger than can be imagined. To my horror I saw that people were going to the fire; these people were not happy at all. They were fighting, bitter, angry and crying. It was the most devastating scene I had ever witnessed. Jesus told me that this fire was coming for those who are not saved. "The end of their life will be in this fire." He spoke solemnly and there was much sadness in His eyes.

The next thing I knew, we were standing in what would be the last place shown me. It was an entrance to somewhere. Before entering Jesus stopped. Turning to me He gently and so powerfully spoke words I will always remember, "Look at My scarred hands, they were nailed to the cross. My own body was sacrificed for you. I shed my blood on that cross for people to be saved." His words echoed in my spirit like the peals of thunder that follow the closest of lightning. I looked again at this Man who was God Himself and was immediately undone by His unfathomable love.

Standing there in front of that mysterious entrance Jesus kept looking at me tenderly and said, "It is not time for you to enter this house. It is time for you to go back." There was no arguing with Jesus because immediately at this point I was back. I was stunned to see myself in my own home. "What is this?" the words tumbled out of my shocked self. I looked around the familiar room, everything was in its place as if nothing extraordinary had happened. I wiggled my toes, stretched my fingers and blinked my eyes trying to collect all that had just happened to me. The morning's disaster at the festival slipped back into my mind, *The rock on my head. The welt that throbbed so terribly... but wait, I feel fine!* I thought to myself. I shook my head and gingerly reached up to feel for the tender spot but found, to my great surprise, that not only was the pain gone but also the swelling too. All of it had mysteriously disappeared! I lay there looking up at the roof, I felt so different than ever before. I knew that in meeting Jesus, my whole world had just changed!

**Gideon's Bible**

The eventful day wasn't quite complete for there was one more surprise waiting to be found. It was closer than I could imagine. I swung my legs off the side of the bed and sat up, in doing so I saw an unfamiliar book resting at the head of the bed. *That's strange!* I thought, *There's never been a book like that in our hut.* Looking closer I opened the front page to discover it was a Bible. Being a pagan family, we had never had a Bible in our home. I gingerly picked it up. It wasn't a new book by any means, and written in freehand along the outer edge was the name Gideon. I had never met anyone named Gideon before. Certainly no one in my village had this name. Where did it come from?

Nobody ever claimed this Bible or admitted to placing it there on my bed that day. The secret of how it got there remains a mystery. Nevertheless, however He accomplished it, God brought His Word straight into my life.

Thankfully my head felt just fine, but sitting there in the house I was confused. Heaven's reality remained mere minutes behind me, I had enjoyed being with

Jesus so much. I couldn't understand why I had to come back to earth. I asked questions in the following days to a few people in the village. I tried my best to describe to them what had happened but was always met with skeptical looks and shrugging shoulders. They didn't understand me at all.

"I know the plans I have for you." God's word tells us in Jeremiah 29:11. God has such wonderful plans for all who say yes to Him. We might not understand at first but He always knows what is best for us and what will make our life in Him most complete and purposeful here on earth.

## On the way to heaven

In spite of all the times that Habbakuk had spotted me when I hadn't wanted him to, I found that in the days following my encounter with Jesus, no matter how hard I looked the evangelist was nowhere to be seen. As the weekend approached I knew in my heart that I wanted to go to the previously avoided christian church. Habbakuk would be there and my hope was that if I went to the church he could help me learn more about this Person I had met named Jesus.

Nevertheless, my desire to go to the church was hindered by just one problem. For as long as I could remember every weekend I worked full days with my father on our sugar cane and water yam farm. With all the work there was to do on the farm I couldn't imagine him agreeing for me to take the time off to go anywhere, let alone attend a christian church service. My father was a hard worker and he depended on my help. If I wanted to leave the work, even a mere suggestion of abandoning the farm would have normally landed me a lashing.

I still didn't know hardly a thing about God, and don't know why I decided I could still have conversations with Him. Certainly I had no idea what prayer was. However, while I might not have known how to pray, that week I found myself asking my new Friend in heaven to help me talk with my Papa. Strangely

I found that talking to Jesus on earth came as naturally to me as it had felt when I had spoken with Him in heaven. As the days slipped by and the weekend loomed ahead, I finally decided to be bold and ask Papa for Sunday morning off. It may have been a courageous thing to do, but I still felt afraid. I wasn't expecting his reply to be in my favor, and therefore I was completely surprised when Papa's response was positive. He agreed immediately without even asking a single question. I was blown away! For the first time in my life, I experienced an answer to prayer without even knowing I was praying. I was so happy!

**New Life**

Sunday couldn't come fast enough, I was so excited to find out more about Jesus. Early on Sunday morning I headed for the church; I was excited and nervous but knew exactly where to go as the sound of praise and worship could be heard from quite a distance away. The music joyfully danced its way across the morning breeze. That first walk to church was years ago now, but I still can clearly recall the sound as I walked up to the front door of the sanctuary. The words of the song they were singing were so hopeful and bright, "We are traveling to the Lord. We are on our way to heaven."

The name of the church was Heaven's Vessel. I felt confident that I was in the right place. The joy in my heart mixed together with a few butterflies as I stepped inside not knowing one clue what to do once I was there. Thankfully, I was greeted very warmly by my friends Charles, James, Eric, and others. The value of kindness no matter how small or simple the gesture should never be underestimated. I quickly felt very comfortable in this welcoming atmosphere. There was a lot of laughing, clapping, and a lot of happiness coming my way. Almost before I realized it, all those butterflies had flown away!

"Are you here for a visit alone, or are you here to join us in worshiping the Lord forever?" This was the first question I was asked. Confidently I responded "Yes, I want to worship the Lord forever." Habbakuk was there and he was perhaps more surprised and delighted than anyone to see me. He called me to the front for prayer and led me in the best words to pray. I gladly repeated the simple prayer and accepted Jesus as my Lord and Savior. It was the best decision in my life to ask Jesus into my heart.

What an amazing reality that through the love of God, I went in that one second of saying 'yes' to all that Jesus freely offered, from darkness to light, death to life. Praise Jesus! My hopeless existence gave way to a hope filled forever. Nevertheless, on my mortal side of life I also had to face a very sneaky, though fleeing enemy and he had to be dealt with. It was integral to take authority over this enemy in Jesus name and make sure he obeyed and let me go according to the Word of God!

And so it happened later that same day my new Christian friends lovingly prayed to God for my deliverance from the enemy's darkness. Blood covenants that had been attached to my life from infancy needed to be broken off and cast out. Kind hands were felt on my shoulders and head as they began to pray in Jesus' name breaking every witchcraft curse and demonic stronghold that was active in my life. Jesus' power is so much greater than the chains that would have liked to keep me prisoner. The prayers were simple, and passionate. God listened and answered. The enemy had no choice but to comply, it was a real deliverance!

In the physical I started sweating and began to vomit a horrible black substance, fortunately we were outside at the time. This looked terrible but it was exactly what needed to happen. All credit to Jesus, the many demonic strongholds over my life lifted that day. I felt the heavy weight of darkness that had become so normal give way to the light of God. Jesus was my Savior and He was so faithful to deliver me. I felt wonderfully free inside my spirit, I knew that I was a son of God and He was to forever be my heavenly Papa. Yes, my new life had begun and the future before me had never looked so bright.

Shortly after this, I was baptized in one of the rivers that flowed past our village.

I wanted the world to know how much God loved me and how I loved Him too. While the days ahead would involve sacrifice in my life in order to follow Jesus, I found and continue to find that no cost will ever be too high after receiving what He has to freely offer us. Nothing compares to the sacrifice Jesus made. In a heaven of perfection He came down to our earth full of pain and scooped up broken humanity, into His capable, forgiving and loving arms. He chose to selflessly give His life for us and in doing this He demonstrated for all eternity that God is Love. As the days to come would unfold in their unusual ways God continued to be my stability in all the times of shaking and in all the times of rest.

**New name**

The sun was beating down in its relentless way one bright afternoon as Charles and I went running past the church building. In the doorway stood one of the elders holding an important looking book. He called us over and asked if we would sit down for a minute. After the customary greetings the elder proceeded with his request, "Okay, now tell me your full names and I'll write them right here in the church record." The elder pointed with emphasis, tapping seriously on his notebook. He went on to explain to us how he was filling in the names of all the church members, every individual's name must be recorded correctly. He poised his pen as Charles, who is most honest, started dutifully spelling out his name.

Waiting my turn I found my mind beginning to think real hard. I had recently been reading the book of Revelation; so full of strange and awesome events. Woven among the incredible chapters was one unbeatable angel named Michael, I was intrigued and in awe of him. Sitting there on the wooden bench inside the church my legs began to swing a little faster, kicking up the dust covered floor. I was absorbed watching the little particles swirl this way and that imagining all the victories Angel Michael triumphed in for the Kingdom of God. With these thoughts racing through my mind a brilliant, though not so honest, idea sprung into my head. *Now, if only I can say what I need to say courageously,* I reasoned to myself.

"Okay, now your turn." The voice was Charles as he poked me out of my daydreaming. I jumped up and began, "My name is..." I breathed in for added emphasis and courage, "My name is Angel Michael Bentum." The man looked up at me and frowned, "What?" he asked quizzically, "I thought your name was Kofi, now please, what do you want me to write in the record?" "Well..." my initial boldness was quickly beginning to wane, "Well, you can call me Angel Michael or Michael Bentum. One of those will be my name from here on going."

The more I thought about it the more I seriously embraced this new name and was proud to have the courage to stick with it. I looked intently at the elder with just a little frown of my own to show him my sincerity, or perhaps, just in the hopes to see if he even believed one word of what I had just said. Lifting his pen he smiled, "Alright my boy, Michael Bentum it is then." And that was that. This new name further punctuated the new person I had become. Somewhat surprisingly, and of the logistics I have no clue, but the name Michael totally stuck. I was Michael not just to those around the village but also to every person I met from then on, in addition to all legal documents I own, including my birth certificate.

**Growing in Christ**

Although we had known each other as friends for as many years as we could think of, Charles, James, Eric, and I quickly became close brothers in Christ. At first we were shy to sing, shy to talk about Jesus or pray in front of others but gradually we became more confident in our christian expressions.

Habbakuk, the evangelist who initially had reached out to us all with the love of Jesus, really stepped up and adopted us as his sons in the Lord. He spent many hours teaching us numerous things from the Bible about how to live the christian life. We learned how to read the Bible, pray, worship and sing.

This practical education is something I will always remember and greatly appreciate. Habakkuk was a gifted musician and God really used his gift to bless all who heard him praising Jesus. He was incredibly talented with his voice and instruments and encouraged us to practice and use the gifts God had placed in our own lives. While we all loved to sing it quickly became evident that Charles had a real talent in this area of music. And so he became a worship leader at the church and to this day leads out in music everywhere he goes. Charles not only expresses and blesses others with his music but he loves to teach others to grow in their musical talents as well.

Prayer became like our daily food. We found ourselves joining the church at the start of a year of all-night prayer meetings. We joined right in and devoted ourselves to pray every night from ten in the evening until four in the morning. The location chosen was called State Park and just so happened to be the village's football field. To many Christians these prayer meetings may be viewed as excessive but this was Africa and this is what we did. Lack of sleep was a small price to pay in my pursuit of Jesus.

Occasionally, the caretaker for the ball field would come around in those dark night hours and spot us praying. We had to be careful of this man because often he was drunk and would chase us with his stick, wielding it our way until we were run right out of the field. Instead of getting upset at the man, we were encouraged to start praying for him instead. Over time he softened towards us. And then one memorable night the caretaker accepted Jesus as his Savior. Soon after this he became an evangelist, fully dedicated to leading others to Jesus in the communities of Ghana.

**Holy Spirit's refreshing rain**

I did not pray in tongues. But neither was I opposed to this gift from Holy Spirit, it was desired by my friends and I. Surrounded by some who did have a prayer language, my friends and I were eager for this gift but not impatient. I waited in hopeful expectation. The absence of ability didn't discourage us in our praying for we knew God was good and would make things beautiful in His time. God looks at our hearts, not just our ability. A prayer topic would be shared by one person and all of us would join in a chorus of praying together. Oftentimes we would pray this way for one hour straight before continuing on to another subject.

When our words in the local language of Twi were exhausted, or we did not know how to pray for a certain situation we would simply start saying Jesus name over and again. Jesus is so powerful, even when we do not know what to pray we can declare His name. I love the song that says, "There is power in the name of Jesus, it breaks every chain." I desired the baptism of the Holy Spirit and my heart was open for God to fill me fully. God is a good Father, loving to bless His children with every good gift. And so it was at the perfect time, Holy Spirit baptized me in His love and I received from Him my personal prayer language.

I do not recall the exact day, but I clearly remember how this precious moment in my life took place. It happened during one night of prayer just as the rain began to fall on us. Rain falling was not an uncommon occurrence in the least. In fact, in the country of Ghana we get lots of rain; however, on this particular night as the rain covered my head in those big wet raindrops, I felt a shower of God's Presence and His love wash right over me. Not just over me like a blanket but also in and around filling me up completely. As the rain kept falling I found myself praying in a language I had not learned before. There was no struggle or striving, it was simply a gracious gift that was given, it had come like refreshing rain from the Father. It was not like some outside force came bearing down on my vocal chords either, but rather a joy that simply bubbled up from inside me and overflowed effortlessly out of my mouth. It was the first time the love and adoration I had for God deep within my spirit, and for which I previously had no words, came spilling over in heavenly expression as the Holy Spirit helped me.

It was not difficult to pray this way but rather the most natural prayer I had ever experienced. Through the blessing of Holy Spirit I gratefully received this gift from God. Tongues continue to be a gift I treasure deeply and use often. In life there are constantly moments and situations where I use my personal prayer language. Praying in the Spirit gives voice to the gratitude and love for God that my heart longs to express. It also provides an avenue for the right prayers to be prayed, especially in times where my own ideas or thoughts could come in the way of what really needs to be prayed.

Recently my parents had divorced and I was now living with my father and stepmother. During the year of nightly prayer, I would often come home in the morning only to have either my father or stepmother say, "When you come home, there's a fire around you." I could not disagree with them because Jesus living inside of me was just like a fire that warmed me up bringing so much hope, joy and peace to my life. Unfortunately however, the comments at my home were never intended as a compliment but rather they were stated as a frustrating matter of fact. I was worried about the reactions I was beginning to receive. Daily life was becoming increasingly tense in my home environment. While the fire of God burned brightly in my heart warming my soul there was an altogether different kind of fire about to break out. I could almost smell the smoke of this new fire as it kindled in the shadows. I did not know how soon it was about to explode, bringing a change that would affect the remainder of my childhood.

# Chapter 5 - Home No More

**"Even if my father and mother abandon me,
the Lord will hold me close."
~ Psalm 27:10 NLT ~**

H ow can a heart be so full of joy and pain all at the same time? I squeezed my eyes tightly shut not wanting a single teardrop to escape, this was the question I simply couldn't avoid anymore. Deep inside my spirit I knew the answer and the knowledge of it pained me all the more. It hadn't taken very long at all to recognize that my newfound faith in Jesus Christ was not only foreign to my family but was by facts alone completely in opposition to the entire life they embraced and believed in. As my relationship with Jesus grew, I saw only disdain and fear coming from my family. The reality that I now followed God was too much for them and the enemy quickly began creating an impassable chasm between my parents and I.

These smoldering embers burst into a fiery confrontation one starkly memorable day. I arrived home from a prayer meeting at State Park only to have my stepmother meet me at the door screaming, "Get out of this house!" In a violent rage she hurled a basin of black water in my direction. It was in vain that I attempted to duck, the harsh spray of poisonous water splashed across my face. Stumbling backwards down the step I tried to wipe the nasty concoction out of my eyes. I knew things were tense at home but I didn't know how bad it was until this moment. I ran from the house, not knowing where to go but only knowing I had no choice but to leave.

While not particularly common, Her actions were not unknown to me. She had chosen one of the preferred ways in our region to take away the life of an enemy. The water she had purchased was costly and bought from the witch doctor. Custom made poison through ugly incantations and ingredients. While to some this action would quickly signify the start of certain death, I thank God that He covered me in the protection of Jesus' blood at that time. By God's grace I did not die or even become sick.

## Forgiveness - jumping forward to look back

It was many years after this incident that God spoke to me about the necessity of forgiving my stepmother. I had long before forgiven my parents and hardly gave a thought to my stepmother as I had never developed a close relationship with her. However, there remained a seed of hurt. Small though it was, it stubbornly hung on. Holy Spirit wanted to uproot this from my heart. Having committed my life entirely to God I did not want anything to come between my relationship with Him or the destiny which He had for me. I remember how gently the Lord revealed to my heart the importance of forgiving this lady who had been such a key player during those early days of rejection and abuse.

There was nothing outwardly to confess, as I had not retaliated towards her in any verbal or physical way. But Holy Spirit showed me how withholding forgiveness towards this woman was imprisoning not only her, but my own heart as well.

In the grace of God and after much prayer, I went to her one day as she was sitting with my father in the old village house. In that place I released to her my forgiveness for which she had never asked. It was a gift God's love alone enabled me to give and my stepmother was blown away. With many tears she stood up from her chair and embraced me inside the very same house where years before she had tried to curse my life and destroy me. It was a profoundly grace filled moment for both of us. My act of radical obedience towards God gave her the capacity to see the love of God.

## Nowhere to go

But stepping back to that day when it all fell apart, I knew, beyond any shadow of doubt, that my father's home was no longer mine. I also knew it was not possible to return to my mother's home. My mother is a practical woman and to her credit, she was still raising my four younger siblings, all of whom were under 12 years of age. Also, if they weren't more than enough for her to care for, she now had a brand new set of twins from another relationship. With at least seven in her tiny one room hut, I was not welcome back.

On the cusp of becoming a teenager I now found myself homeless. It was certainly a vicious blow to my childhood. There was no time to brood over the brutal reality of having to step into life on the streets alone. *Where will I safely sleep? Where will I eat next?* Yet praise God He kept the fire in my heart burning for Jesus and He was there to provide for me. I thank God, He will never leave us, truly He remained by my side giving me the courage and the strength to face this loss.

While rejected by my parents and not welcome to enter their homes, I didn't entirely lose contact with my family as we all still remained in the small village. My sister Essi, who was quite a few years older than I and had her own home, began in a small way to watch out for me. Although I never stayed with her, Essi would at times give me a meal in exchange for helping her sell fresh cooked rice in the market. And surprising though it may appear, I also continued helping my father with his sugar cane farm. After the incident with the poison he had sided with my stepmother, and certainly did not agree with my new life. Papa nevertheless still had some sense of obligation towards me as his firstborn son and would sometimes allow me to take a small portion of water yams and cane to sell in exchange for helping him on the farm. Every small income was vital to me as I was learning how to survive in those days.

At night I stayed outside under the stars, usually in State Park. Even at 12 years of age I quickly learned how to accommodate the hard ground and multitude of mosquitoes buzzing voraciously around. Sometimes the drenching rain would beat my body so much that it became impossible to try and sleep. How delighted I was to find a very small wooden shed called a kiosk in the village. One of the local women used the shed during the day to do ladies hair and so the shed was filled with all her salon products. I wasn't interested in any of that, but I most certainly was interested in her kind offer of allowing me to sleep there on those extra rainy nights. After she left in the evening I would slip inside the empty shop for shelter from the rain. It leaked a little and the mosquitoes always found their way inside, but I slept there dry and warm, waking early enough to leave before the woman arrived. I used this shed for about three years. Through every day and mosquito swarming night God protected me. Malaria is a very real threat in Africa and yet, miraculously, not even once in my entire life have I contracted this sickness.

Even as my family kept me at a distance, Papa God remained so close. He is such a faithful Father, I found my love for Him growing by leaps and bounds. In the midst of all the turmoil Holy Spirit leaned in close to comfort me and kept my heart in a safe place. I was grateful to have a church family close by and brothers in Christ to walk with me during those early days of navigating childhood on my own.

**On the edge of a coming storm**

After so much disaster on my own home front, I wish it could be said that the spiritual environment around me remained a safe place. I wish I could tell you that the church I had come to call home of sorts continued to be a stable ground of encouragement, and unshakable friendships. This was not to be. If there's one thing we soon learn in life, it is that friends will and do so often fail us.

I also learned that Jesus is unfailing and He is a faithful friend. As I kept trusting

Jesus, He walked me through every difficulty. Wherever I went, whatever came my way, Jesus was my stability and security.

And so it was that things were once more about to change radically in my world. This time they would take such a dramatic spin in one of the most weird ways imaginable. To this day I thank God for how carefully He walked me through it all at such an impressionable young age.

# Chapter 6 - The Strangest Demise

*"In that day He will be your sure foundation,*
*providing a rich store of salvation, wisdom and knowledge.*
*The fear of the Lord will be your treasure."*
*~ Isaiah 33:6 NLT ~*

S haking our heads in dismay James, Eric, and I stared in confused shock as Charles unraveled the disturbing details of what had happened. "Are you serious? How can it be?" we asked again in disbelief.

With grief and in horror we sadly came to know that it really was true. Habbakuk, our christian mentor, friend, and one of the most passionate evangelists whom God had so recently used to touch our lives, traded light for darkness and literally lost his mind. How in the world had this happened?

Often Habbakuk would hike to the mountains for fasting and prayer, each time returning with so much joy and fresh grace in his life. He would help us grow spiritually and was always eager to read to us from the Bible. Often in his reading he would stop to burst out singing a song, joyfully urging us to join in and worship Jesus with him. We all looked up to Habbakuk which is why we were so devastated to learn just how much, and how quickly, everything changed for him.

Without revealing to anyone his true motives, he and Charles had taken a trip to a neighboring village. The two of them stayed the night with a woman who called herself a prophet of God. Early the next morning Charles had left the woman's house and returned home. But even as he walked away he couldn't help frowning over the words he had heard come from this lady's mouth. Something wasn't right about what she had spoken. It bothered him that Habbakuk was still there at her home. "Thank goodness he's also leaving today!" Charles fully expected the evangelist was soon to be going on his way to pray in the mountains.

As it turned out, however, Habbakuk never continued on to the mountains. Instead of journeying to his prayerful retreat like he had informed everyone, he stayed with the woman. It is not known how our friend connected with her in the first place, but a prophet of God she was not. She simply used this false identity to deceive Habbakuk into trusting her. Habbakuk fell headlong into the enemy's plot. Each moment at the woman's home created an open door for darkness.

How is this possible? All it took was one tiny lie to crack the door. He had told everyone that he was going to pray on a mountain top when instead he was planning a visit in the valley with this false prophet. Even Charles who journeyed with him, was told that it was merely a stopover visit on the way to the mountain and he, Charles, must go home. Why was Habbakuk being so secretive?

This woman had told Habbakuk that she had a special message for him. The message was the word that Charles heard her speaking as he was leaving the house. While Charles couldn't say exactly why the words so troubled his spirit, concern him they did as he made his way home. The woman had declared that the Lord had informed her that she should put salt in Habbakuk's hands and have him raise them to the sky. Once raised in the air she wanted to then pray for him. Simplistic it may seem but this act was not of God, it was fully demonic. The specific details are lost in the absence of any person being there to witness firsthand what took place after Charles left. But the results of this encounter were tragically obvious to all; and they were immediate for our friend. Habbakuk must have complied with the woman, allowing her to do everything that she spoke so confidently of. He immediately lost his mind that day and was never the same again.

The woman was some sort of witch doctor, juju or fetish priest, it need not matter to us other than to say she was not a prophet and certainly not of God. When Habbakuk willingly went along with the request, without first praying about it or seeking wisdom from others, she was able to use this act with the salt to curse the evangelist. Upon leaving her home he started to climb the small hills around the village. Madness drove him to climb them over and over day after day and sometimes ten times per day as the voices he babbled on about directed him. Habbakuk's clothing quickly became ragged, stinky and worn. His physical appearance barely resembling the man he used to be.

It was a devastating fall and a tragic loss. Many times we tried to reach out to Habbakuk. The pastor provided clothes for him and yet he would wear only one piece for sometimes a month at a time. The love and mercy of God would surely have broken every curse over Habbakuk's life, and yet tragically, he opposed every available grace and forgiveness. He was not willing for prayers of deliverance and nothing we attempted to do for him was ever received.

**Purging from the pulpit**

With Habbakuk gone, we became closer friends with our senior pastor. He was a very well-liked pastor when we first met him. In addition to Heaven's Vessel church, he had successfully planted two other churches in the general area. He welcomed each of us from the first day we arrived and took us under his wing when Habbakuk's downfall became evident.

Some time passed quite peacefully before this pastor of ours became close friends with a teenager in the church named Atta. At first my friends and I envied Atta, he seemed like a son to the pastor and was constantly talking so confidently about almost any subject. All the same, our envy was short lived when Atta began to tell the pastor, "This person in your church is a witch! That person is a witch!"

For reasons that I do not know, our pastor completely went along with Atta's lying accusations and foolishly believed every word Atta would say. Instead of seeking God in prayer, counseling with elders, or going to each person individually, our senior pastor would expel them from the church premise, publicly and quickly. Often with the parting words, "You are a witch. Leave now!" This caused a lot of confusion and angst among the members that remained as well as the ones who were told to leave. It wasn't long before the other two churches lost so many members via this ill-advised and un-Christlike method, that they shut down totally. The rapid demise would soon include our own church as well. The local community was so upset with what was happening that they came into the church building one Sunday, armed with sticks and very angry. In no time at all they had chased the pastor right out the door of his own church. It was an absolutely ridiculous time in my life.

Our church was no longer soul winning, but rather member purging. It got to the point where all who were left in membership with our pastor were Atta, my friends Incum, James, Kofi, Charles, Eric, and I. Nine of us with no longer a church building to meet in. Our vastly dwindling group began to meet at the pastor's home for church each week.

One would surely hope after all this that the light would come on for the pastor, nevertheless, his literal witch hunt was not over yet. All Atta would have to say was, "Pastor, I've seen something." And our gullible pastor always urged him on, "Atta, tell us the truth!" Week by week our group got smaller and smaller. Kofi left, then Incum left, next went James, followed by Eric. Each in turn was kicked out and told that they were witches and were therefore going to die. Charles and I were the last ones remaining alongside our pastor and Atta. We were stunned and we felt stuck.

Let me stop right here. What was it that kept my friend Charles and I tagging along with such an obviously misguided pastor, especially as all our close friends were told to leave? It almost goes without saying that after leaving, our brothers were so furious at the lies and injustice of it all they would have nothing to do with us anymore. Why didn't we stand up and leave such nonsense? These are very good questions and can perhaps be answered in part by understanding the following; from a very young age we were taught to have the utmost respect for authority. This concept permeates our African culture and was not something we learned from the church alone. Children especially are expected to have respect for parents and elders in the village and everyone is obliged to respect the village chief above all. We were taught to lavish great honor to whomever was over us. This cultural respect usually had no correlation to whether the person was deserving of it or not. Respect was a duty, it was just what we did in life. While we began to question many things, we had not come to the place of breaking away from this cultural reality. Therefore, in spite of his irresponsible actions, respecting our pastor was the ingrained thing to do. He was our authority, much older than both of us, but also, over us as our spiritual leader. So holding to the culture we were raised to follow we felt obliged to stay with him.

While his current behavior was so blatantly bizarre, a quick look back at our short history told us that we had a lot to thank this man for. Still fresh in our minds was the way in which our pastor had helped us, how he had welcomed us into the fellowship of family at a time when physical family life was falling apart. He was one of our first christian mentors and from this man we had learned to appreciate and memorize the Bible. He had spent hours instilling in us the importance of faith in Jesus. All these were very tangible blessings he gave. Charles and I were both young and homeless and so we clung to him as a father, and we respected him as such. The fact that he had fallen into a life of lies and critical judgement was troubling to both Charles and I. In our confusion we found ourselves faced with a question neither of us could answer; how could we reject our own pastor, who hadn't even rejected us? Not yet anyway. So it was at the end of our concerns we yielded our loyalties to him, waiting to see what would come next.

## Time to take a stand

"The weather is so perfect we're going to meet outside today." I told Charles as he joined our small group. "Yes boys, in fact I know of just the place." Our pastor smiled radiantly as he launched out in front. Off the four of us strode straight into a day like none other before. Unbeknown to me at that moment, it would be a day of loss but also a day of great freedom and victory in my life of knowing and following Jesus.

With all the events of recent months, it was good to be outside in God's fresh air. Breathing deeply I prayed inwardly, 'Praise You Lord for the reliable air.' We passed over a makeshift bridge before hiking up a little hill and emerging into a quiet sunshiny spot. Banana palms sprung up at odd intervals and a large tree stood to one side of the clearing. We sat down under the tree's shade and made ourselves comfortable. "Perfect place!" Atta declared; I nodded in agreement.

Not long after we had settled ourselves, a big black bird started singing in the tree right over our heads. In Ghana there is a very common black bird, about the size of a large crow and perhaps they're cousins. This particular variety of bird has a sharp black mouth and is covered in thick, inky black feathers, all except for its chest which is contrasted with feathers of solid white. The birds look smart and stylish in their feathery tuxedos but nonetheless they are a cheeky bird and hardly live up to their refined looks. This particular bird started to sing and right there with the start of his song is where the real story of this pivotal day begins.

Upon hearing the bird, our pastor stopped talking and turned his full attention towards me. He asked casually, "Michael, what is the bird saying?" I didn't have to ponder the answer for nobody knows what birds say, unless of course they're listening to a talking parrot. This bird was no talking parrot, only a cheeky black bird cackling his own unknown tune. But as for the question itself? It was very strange. I frowned and looked over towards Charles before replying, "Pastor, I don't know what the bird is saying!" Thinking this to be some sort of joke I smiled bemusedly waiting to see his response.

Instead of smiling back our pastor instantly lost his pastoral poise. With a lungful of irritation in his voice he yelled at me, "Michael, you are a liar! The bird is throwing weapons at us!" Turning his attention to Charles he asked the same question again, "Charles, what is the bird saying?" *How could our pastor actually be serious?* Charles and I didn't know what to make of this sudden diversion from a worshipful morning. Perplexed at what all seemed so silly to us we both began to laugh. This did not help the situation - exasperated, I spoke up, "We don't know!" Charles quickly joined in, "That's right, only God knows what the bird is saying!" The look of disgust on our pastor's face indicated to us clearly that the birds antics were very real to him. To us on the other hand it was increasingly ridiculous.

Next the same question was posed to Atta, but he just sat there refusing to reply. The pastor let loose a fury of rage and then said, "Atta, tell the truth!" So Atta caved in and said, "The birds are throwing weapons." Pleased with Atta's reply the pastor paused for just a moment before going on, "Atta, I'm about to ask you a question. Tell the truth! Are Michael and Charles witches?" Again Atta kept quiet. In a violent lashing out of words our pastor shouted, "Tell the truth Atta!" And then Atta nodded, "Yes pastor, they are witches." he said in agreement. "See?!" Screamed the pastor in a weird tone of triumph, "Atta has confirmed my discernment. You two are both witches and will surely die for it."

Reeling at the absurdly disastrous turn of our peaceful morning and the escalating rage of our senior pastor, we simply sat there with wide eyes and open mouths. How should we respond? How could we respond? We had seen this happen to all the others before, but now it was our turn to be blamed as witches. Face to face with our accuser we sat there, the air still ringing with those unfortunate lying words. Words of deception the pastor had foolishly allowed to overtake his mind. No human response was sufficient enough to verbally extract ourselves from this senseless circumstance.

We were desperate for wisdom from Jesus, and like a good Father He was right there to stand with us. In fact, right at that very moment Holy Spirit dropped a powerful and needed passage of scripture straight into my brother Charles' thoughts. Not only did Holy Spirit bless Charles with the thought, but also, in that critical junction Charles was filled with the courage to stand and speak up to the pastor like he had never done before. Out of Charles' mouth came the strategic and timely words declared with heavenly boldness. He spoke them straight to the pastor and Atta:

"Let a man so consider us, as servants of Christ and stewards of the mysteries of God. Moreover it is required in stewards that one be found faithful. But with me it is a very small thing that I should be judged by you or by a human court."

Charles stopped, waiting for the heaven sent words to strike home before he went on confidently:

"In fact, I do not even judge myself. For I know of nothing against myself, yet I am not justified by this; but He who judges me is the Lord!"

It was a passage from 1 Corinthians 4.1-4 God had given the words and they fit perfectly for our current predicament. The Word of God was powerful and lifted us right out of the pit we were in. Going by the look on the pastor's face the words obviously had met their mark. Unfortunately the thoughtful look on his face soon disappeared and he went back to his initial anger. Waving an accusing finger at Charles he roared, "Charles, you are quoting me!" To this Charles immediately replied, "No pastor I am not quoting you, this is the word of God." I could feel the same courage from Holy Spirit taking hold in my own heart and I boldly joined in, "Pastor, the word of God is our helmet. If this bird is throwing things and hits you with an arrow then it means you are not wearing the armor He has given."

Our pastor stood looking at us in silence and shock, trying desperately to regain his religious solemness. Clearing his throat he said with poised disgust, "You've surprised me. Michael, Charles, you have both surprised me! Since my ministry began nobody has questioned me, or spoken to me, or surprised me like you both have done today!"

By this time the two of us were standing up. We did not reply and neither were we about to take back the words the Lord had given to confront the pastor with. Upon seeing repentance was far from arriving, our pastor said, "Okay, you people can go. If you two don't accept what I am saying, leave."

We were so ready to leave. Picking up our bibles we did just that, we left. Initially we were extremely mad at Atta for all his lies and we made no delay in telling him so as he trailed behind us that day. Our immaturity was made evident when we threatened to drown him at the river bridge on our way back to the village, but we thank God for quickly restraining our hot and immature tempers. We all made it safely back to town. Consistent with the weirdness of this season the final moments were equally bizarre. We knew the ties had been severed and we were happy to move on.

Clearly, it was after this incident that our freedom in Christ began to blossom. No more would we remain silently sitting like immobile little robots, bending and swaying to another person's control just for the sake of misguided 'respect'. We began to understand like never before that we must know Jesus and know His Word for ourselves. Honoring and respecting our Papa God in heaven must always be our highest goal. All too well Charles and I had just learned the painful lesson of honoring man to extremely unhealthy places. I want to emphasize that honor for others, in its rightful place, is not wrong. In fact, honor is a strong principle and one that comes through very clearly in the Bible. However, when misguided honor lifts up another human to places of authority over us that God never intended we quickly find ourselves falling into a dangerous quicksand. For Charles and I we had lost the true essence of honor and had instead become pleasers of man and not of God. This will always lead to serious trouble.

I thank God for His grace. He really does understand every detail of our lives and how easily circumstances can tangle us up like in a spiders web. How carefully Jesus had reached down and extracted Charles and I from where we had unsuspectingly ended up. What a relief it was to find ourselves untangled and free to honor God above man and find our freedom in Him.

Truly God works all things out for our good as we allow Him to navigate the treacherous terrains of the unexpected. I don't believe God caused all the upheavals and oddities of those early years one bit; however, I do believe God used that journey through many losses, as a pathway to great gains. At the end of those days I had found my stable refuge in Jesus Christ alone. I started to understand God's value for me even as I learned far deeper to value Him first and foremost in my life.

When what I knew was ripped away, when the structures around me began to crumble and so many to whom I had looked up to also stumbled and fell, Jesus remained. He remained more than enough and His grace continually held me. Yes, I had lost my earthly family only to go on and lose my church family but through all the craziness God held my hand and led me through. One of my favorite songs says it best of all, "On Christ the Solid Rock I stand, All other ground is sinking sand!" If there's one thing I learned it is this, I could confidently take my stand in Jesus, for He had already promised to make His home in me.

# Chapter 7 - Days of Purpose

"We give thanks to You, O God, we give thanks.
For Your wondrous works declare that Your name is near."
~ Psalm 75:1 ~

I t wasn't overnight that friendships were restored between Charles, myself, and our christian brothers but as soon as the opportunity arose to make amends we did so. God graciously brought about a profound restoration between us all. How good if felt to once again be surrounded with like minded friends who were honestly seeking to follow Jesus and know Him more.

Right about this time one of the churches, in a neighboring town called Adum, began to hold a nondenominational prayer meeting each week. Weekly trips to Adum via bus for prayer soon became our habit as we joined in praying with a variety of Christians from the surrounding churches. We prayed for our families, villages, our country and the world. There were a lot of people who came to this weekly service and on some occasions we would even see our old senior pastor. Without fail he always acted surprised to see us and would sometimes say, "You still don't believe me?" attempting to remind us of his former words over our lives. We held our mouths shut and did not respond to these antagonizing pricks. Instead, we reminded ourselves that we were there for God not man. Whatever this man's motives were in coming to the prayer, or in trying to discourage us, were not to be our concern. We gave it all to God in prayer.

However, while this pastor's actions, past or present, weren't our concern it was a concern for someone else looking on. One of the pastors who attended the prayer meeting from a nearby church named Living Bread somehow heard about what had happened to our previous church and he was very concerned. As soon as he found out that we were the remaining group of boys with no church to belong to he quickly came to ask us to come and worship at his church. He continued to encourage us to come, assuring us that we would be cared for well and even provided with a home. His motives may well have been sincere, nevertheless, after all we had gone through with our previous church and pastor, we were at the time extremely wary of joining ourselves to any church. We had a very hard time trusting people and did not feel right about joining this pastor's church. No matter what he said we always kindly declined to accept his offers.

During this season of life as an earliteen, finding food to survive on was very difficult. I knew that if I was not diligent during the day I would be hungry during the day and night. This reality provided motivation to keep searching for odd jobs here and there. Sometimes someone would hire me to do a simple task, such as my older sister Essi with the selling of her rice, or helping my father in his cane and water yam fields. Odd jobs provided fairly well for me, and yet, I still remember the time when there was no money to buy food at all. Charles and I were extremely hungry, our empty stomachs were bitterly complaining. By God's grace it happened to be mango season, so during the early hours of morning, long before daylight we would go quietly into the dark yards of unsuspectingly generous mango owners. We would eat our fill of sweet mangoes until our hungry stomachs settled down. Proverbs 9:17 says, "Stolen water is sweet, food eaten in secret is delicious." We learned it is so true and we also learned that the hungry stomachs of young boys have no conscience.

**Food for thought**

While I was constantly on the lookout for jobs, I probably spent most of my time helping my father with his farm. Farming was something that I had done for many years and I felt very comfortable in those thickly planted fields. While not welcome in the village house I was welcome to help on the farm. Although not as often as it had been in the past, my father and I continued to farm together. On the days that I helped Papa, the longing in my heart for him to know and understand the power of God grew. God's power is so much greater than all other things, it could not even begin to be compared with my father's idols. I prayed to God often for an opportunity to have Papa see for himself the power of God.

One morning my father stood laughing as he saw me coming to join him at the farm, "You always stand somewhere to pray son or you step up on a bank and try and talk about your God to all these people who are coming to buy sugar cane. You want to be a preacher?" his sarcastic laughter echoed across the field. I smiled back at what sounded to me like a fine idea and laughed, "Yes, perhaps I do Papa, perhaps I do." And so began another day where I found myself thinking about how big God was and how Papa was so unaware. Lost in thought I set about working the ground. Later that afternoon when the sun was beating down hard, I struck my machete one last time at an extra tough cane, "That should do it you big thing!" I huffed as the knife cracked successfully through the fibers of the old plant. Watching the cane topple to the ground I wiped the sweat from my forehead and once more began to dream about what a changed man Papa would be if only he could encounter God. *What is there to do?* There it was, the same question finding its place in my thoughts. But this time the question was immediately followed by a brilliant idea. I looked up to heaven and smiled, "That's a perfect idea, thank You God!"

Wasting no time I picked up that large old cane, and walked over to where Papa was busy binding the cut pieces into bundles. "Okay Papa, tell me what you think of this idea. How about you take your idols and plant some sugar cane right here, and I'll take God and plant some cane over there. We'll see which grows the best." It was a sugar cane growing contest, and my father thought it was a terrific idea. We both were certain of the results and eager to see them unfold. I prayed earnestly during those following months as we worked, watched and waited. It wasn't long before the differences between the two fields became dramatically evident. God's side of the field was lush and tall while by significant contrast my father's field grew spindly short canes. There was no mistaking the winner and in good attitude Papa accepted the visible defeat of his idols. He acknowledged that the power of God was capable of growing incredible sugar cane but for reasons unknown to me he remained solid in the hope and pursuit of his idol worship. I couldn't understand this, but I thanked the Lord for the small seed that had been planted in the soil of my father's heart. I prayed for it to grow just like God's sugar cane had.

## Where to hang our hats?

My friends and I, nervous yet optimistic, were now praying to God for a church to go to, we didn't have a clue where this would be as the churches in our village were either nonexistent or pagan ones. A short trip to the bigger surrounding towns posed many options, but which one would be the right one? God was listening and it wasn't long until out of the blue a missions event came right into our very village. Soon the meetings were all set to go in none other than the old State Park.

An American couple were leading out in the meetings. These missionaries to Ghana were joined by other local Ghanaian Christians. Among them were two teenagers, slightly older than ourselves, who set themselves to befriend us. Upon learning that we had no church they began to share with us about their church which surprisingly met in a tent in Kumasi. These two teenage boys were so happy and friendly it wasn't long before our curiosity about them turned to friendship with them. One of the youth was named Charles B. and the other one Thomas.

Not long after the meetings had finished Charles decided to make the bold move to visit their tent church. He was warmly welcomed and thoroughly enjoyed himself. Although, he regarded with fear and suspicion the American missionaries. The couple were older in their years and over time we learned that they had come to our country from the United States as christian missionaries a long time ago.

While we were experiencing greater freedom in many areas of life we still found ourselves fearful of much. For example we truly believed our food could be filled with demons. In fact, if we were eating a meal only one of us would eat while the others would pray. If it took one hour to eat the meal then it came with certainty that we'd pray to Jesus for protection from what may be lingering in our food for that entire hour of eating. This is extreme, especially when considering the fact that we had left our former pastor in part due to his own fear-filled behavior regarding that silly bird. However, while we could now see with clarity many of the lies that our former pastor had us believing, our own hearts still needed greater maturity, wisdom and deliverance. God knew how much our spirits were honestly hungry for truth and it wouldn't be long before that old spirit of fear was gone.

I was curious to hear how it had gone at the tent church for Charles and made a point to meet him on the road home as he returned from his first visit. "Everything was nice! Except for the obruni (Ghanaian term for caucasian) couple who I'm not sure about." Charles told me. "In fact, Thomas and Charles B. met me after the service and they have invited me back. We are all welcome to attend the Tuesday, Friday and weekend services." "Are you going back then?" I asked. "I don't know yet." Charles replied.

Later that same week on our way home from Adum, Charles all at once said, "Michael we should go to the prayer at the tent church, it's tonight. I'm going and will get off the bus at the last roundabout which leads to the tent." I had not been thinking of the tent church and mention of going there made my heart start to beat fast, I just wasn't ready. "No, you go, I'm not going this time." I said. Charles shrugged but I could see he wished I would go with him.

Hesitating just a moment, I added, "I'll come with you on Sunday." Charles hopped off at the roundabout and quickly disappeared down the dimly lit street. Once again he had a wonderful time and this time he even asked if he could sing a song that very next Sunday at the worship. Sunday came and we went together to the tent church, a whole group of us. I was surprised at how accepted and welcomed we were made to feel and how genuine everyone was in their love for Jesus. This was the first of many visits we made and it was not long before all of our friends from Dokojum village started regularly attending the Kumasi tent church. The beginning of a brand new season had started.

**Container of blessing**

"It isn't much boys, but if you're interested you are welcome to move in today." The American missionary pried open the hefty door and tried to brush away the array of cobwebs that greeted us. Beyond the cobwebs lay the dusty interior of a very sturdy shipping container. The rusty red container sat alone in the open grass behind the missionary's home which sat adjacent to the tent church. A few months had passed since my first visit to the church. Over these intervening months I had come to feel fully comfortable and at peace in this new environment. It was a bustling and vibrant new church and there was purpose here for which I could dive straight into with devotion and joy. The journey to and from my village was fine, but as the weeks progressed I knew that it would be so much more convenient staying closer to Kumasi, especially since I didn't even have a home in my village to return to anyway.

Looking over the container that day, no one could have convinced me that it wasn't the best house I had ever seen. To think that it was going to be my home caused me to be even happier. Not only would I be out of the prickly grass in State Park, or temporary hideouts in the hairdresser's shed I now could have a dry place to live located right where I loved to be. Amazing thought! I was delighted and the words burst out of my mouth with no effort at all, "Hallelujah!" I shouted. My shout of joy was joined by six other friends who also planned to call this container home. Among them were Charles,

Eric, James, Frank and our newest friends Charles B and Thomas. While we had to use every square inch just to fit inside the container, it didn't take much time at all to feel right at home in our new quarters. The large mission house had a simple bath house built along one of the outside walls and this provided everything we needed to wash and keep clean. I had never in my life experienced a shower before. Fresh, clean water raining down all around me was incredible, not to mention watching the soap bubbles slip and spin out of sight and down the drain. This sure was a lot nicer than sandy riverbeds, or soap filled bucket baths. These had seen me through the cleanliness of many years but I was completely grateful to God for providing above and beyond.

The container became my home for the next eight years. As those years passed the seven of us who called it home continued to be as close as brothers can be. We did practically everything together, we laughed, cried and ate together, we prayed together, talked for hours and poured ourselves into witnessing and sharing Jesus with all. Also, as we often studied together with the missionary we learned to have a much more mature understanding of some topics we had been previously misguided in. We gratefully let go of the juvenile fears we held as youngsters and our biblical understanding became increasingly balanced even as we matured into our teen years.

## Marshes machetes and miracles

We also saw the tent church grow extensively over those years as more and more people started to come along. They filled the tent week after week until the seams just couldn't hold a single soul more. It was such a vibrant season and full of the goodness of God. As we prayed and sought God for a solution to our minimizing space in the tent we also watched in awe and gratefulness as God touched the lives of so many individuals with generosity and passion for the ministry needs. From the local offerings big and small to the donations from far away in other countries the money started to come trickling in. As the money began to arrive the missionaries faithfully gathered it up until there was enough accumulated to purchase a large block of land only a short walk downhill from the mission compound.

While close to the large town of Kumasi, the new property remained a raw piece of land, swampy and full of snakes. Snakes, all of whom I'm sure were on the lookout for a tasty morsel of one of the innumerable bush meats, slithered here and there through the undergrowth. This place remained empty also because it was a land affected a lot by witchcraft. The demonic atmosphere was so tangible that most people wanted nothing to do with it. And while it is foolish to imagine a boatload of demons added to every plateful of food like my friends and I once were known to do, likewise, it is just as foolish to deny the reality that we are all born into a spiritual war.

Regrettably, this reality of cosmic conflict can oftentimes be played down or sometimes denied altogether in the west. Africa has a long history of being a continent involved in witchcraft. The powers of darkness often blatantly glare one straight in the face and are therefore acknowledged freely by everyone. Jesus is the light to every darkness. He defeated, once and for all, all evil at the cross. Because of what Jesus did we too can be victorious over the enemy in every trial as we live our lives in Him.

Yes, the area may have been dark and heavy but it carried great potential. We were not daunted in the least and encouraged ourselves in the fact that the weapons of our warfare, the promises of God's word, were far sharper than even the blades of our machetes. We moved forward in joy at the beautiful vision of a suitable church building site. There was much to be done on the land by way of clearing and cleaning just in order to make it habitable for a place to start laying the foundation for a church. Long days of sweat and toil always left everyone exhausted, hungry, and sore, but gradually a beautiful transformation began to happen on the land. This spurred us on to greater efforts and prayers for the future finished project.

**Electrical apprenticeship**

As the church building began to take shape, we were so happy. Soon we were ready to put our machetes away and begin laying blocks for the structure. We all knew that God had done great things for the project to have come this far and by His grace the construction would be completed. Shortly after the laying of blocks began an opportunity to study electrical work opened up for me. With the encouragement of my christian family I left the remaining construction of the church to the others and became an apprentice with a local electrician.

My own father was the one to initiate this apprenticeship and I am so grateful that he saw a future for me in this trade. Aside from the disaster some years before, my father still had a heart to see me excel. Truly the grace of God was working in my father's heart. It was because of my father's efforts and word on my behalf that I placed my application with the electrician who would train me over the next five years.

During those five years I was fired by my boss, thankfully only one memorable time. In Ghana there was a custom that if something wrong happened on the job, the apprentice would inevitably take the blame. The boss in almost every account wants to save face, even if it is his wrongdoing. Justifiably, many times there is greater mercy for someone, like an apprentice, who is just learning. But unfortunately, sometimes the boss will deliberately make a miscalculation that profits him a lot of money. In such a case, if the police find out about the dishonest behavior and come to investigate, the boss will quickly blame it all on the apprentice's ignorance. In which case the apprentice will often land in jail initially, only to have the boss come and take him out with little to no questions. At the end of the day the apprentice walks free and the boss walks away all the richer.

One day as my boss put the remaining tools in his bag he gave the parting instruction, "I'm leaving early today Michael, you clear things up and clean around here. I'll see you later." Waving goodbye he headed out and I turned my attention to clearing the job site. It had been a big job and there was much to do. However, the job had not been as big as was quoted to the customer.

Left over from our work was a large coil of expensive wire. This wire was to be taken back to the seller for a full refund and the money returned to the customer. I was just getting ready to stop a local taxi and go return the wire when a message came from my boss, via one of my coworkers to not refund the customer but rather quickly take the wire straight to my boss' house.

To keep the wire was dishonest. A choice must be made to either return the wire and the money, or take the wire to my boss' home. The customer had no idea, it would be easy to get away with this small yet clear dishonesty. On the other hand, failing to obey my boss could very well cost me my apprenticeship. Nevertheless I soon decided to return the wire and refund the money. My firm desire was to honor God, for in the end He was who I was accountable to. He surely knew what my actions would be that day even if nobody else could see. God had cared for me faithfully and my apprenticeship was in His hands not mine. I didn't have to fight for myself. I did not want even the smallest dishonesty to hurt my Papa in heaven.

When the wire failed to arrive at his home and my boss learned that I had disregarded his instructions, everything surrounding me and my apprenticeship became disastrous. He was furious. Calling me to meet with him he exploded, "You're fired!" It was a final blow and there was not a thing I could do to change it. Thankfully, the story of my apprenticeship doesn't finish there because it has a good ending. In Romans 8:31 the question is asked, "If God is for us, who can be against us?" And so it happened that God softened his heart and a short time later, my boss took me back into apprenticeship and I continued with my training. He was a good electrician, an excellent teacher and I thoroughly enjoyed electrical work. Electrical work quickly became my favorite handiwork and is a passion that remains to this day. In the Spring of 2006. I graduated from my apprenticeship and went on to pass all the country's written and technical examinations. I was now a fully licensed Electrician in Ghana ready to start my own electrical work.

**"There's a fire from above!"**

CHAPTER 7 - DAYS OF PURPOSE

God was doing great things in my life, observable and beyond what I could see. A clear example of this came when my father shared with me the following incident. He decided to take a very specific trip to Cape Coast, which happens to be my family's original hometown.

Cape Coast is one of the historic cities in Ghana, it borders the warm waters of the Gulf of Guinea that flow out towards the Atlantic Ocean. This city, though quite a tourist destination now, has a devastating history as one of the primary slave trading ports in West Africa. A massive white castle used as a holding prison for slaves during the many years of slave trading, looms center stage in the city. Its ancient stone walls firmly settled on one of the treacherous rocky ocean cliffs. It was here that the slave trade ships would collect their human 'cargo' from. And so this castle stands as a haunting reminder of a very tragic past. To this day it remains a landmark to which many people from across the world return and visit. It was to this city that my father went.

During this journey to Cape Coast Papa had planned to go to an influential witch doctor and have his children, all seven of us, 'demonically interceded for' by the fetish priest. The intention was to access favor and protection from the gods he worshiped. The appointment was made and without fail the set day arrived. Confidently the witch doctor went about doing all those pagan rites and rituals at my father's request. All was going accordingly with his pagan practices until he came to my name on the list. He tried to start mentioning me but didn't get far. Saying my name that day was not to be. Instead, something most incredible took place as God's goodness took over that dark deed and the unrivaled power of Jesus Christ flooded in to stop the proceedings.

The priest was holding his knife high in the air with one hand when all at once he stopped and said, "No! This one, they don't want to hear his name!" In a sudden shriek of terror and with an ashen face he shouted, "There's a fire from above!" And then, as if the knife had turned to a red hot coal he dropped it. The blade clanged on the cold cement floor even as the fetish priest raced for the door. Darkness couldn't hide, not even in those dark recesses of that

69

witch doctor's office. All the people in the room, my father included, were terrified and raced towards the open door to find cover outside. They couldn't stay inside with the fire of God as it powerfully covered my life once again. "I Myself will be a wall of fire all around…" God faithfully promised Zechariah so many years ago in Zechariah 2:5, and praise His glorious name He is the same for us today.

I am so grateful for God's protection over my life on that day when I was unaware anything was even going on. Knowing of this incident has since made me appreciate the many moments in our lives when God is watching over us. We may never see nor know the intricate details of God's protecting fire as it surrounds our lives but certainly it is there. God is truly the One to fight for us in the battles we see, and in the battles we may never even know about. He is so good. Blessings both tangible and unseen He lavishly poured on my life as the years went on.

# Chapter 8 - As Unto The Lord

**"Whatever you do, do it heartily, as to the Lord"**
**~ Colossians 3:23 ~**

I want to be very honest with you and yet tactful as I share the following realities of my life's journey. The issue I faced was racism. This little word unleashes a battleground full of pain. Many of us have seen with despair from afar or experienced up close its venom. Racism comes in many shades but it all is poison. For me racial prejudice was often, though not always, subtly cloaked in a false guise of condescending care.

While I shifted my focus into learning the electrical trade, my friends continued to put their efforts towards the church construction. Our days were filled to the brim in a variety of ways, nevertheless, many a night was spent together strengthening ourselves in the Lord through prayer, praise and fasting. Our life in Jesus was a passion that we were very sincere about. We knew well that our strength was in Christ alone. Alongside the joys of these busy days there came a struggle that was as real as it was challenging.

It is not my desire to disregard the blessings I received from these missionaries as they poured out their efforts in Ghana, nor lay down a laundry list of sad moments that occurred. I do believe they came to Africa with earnestness in their hearts. I learned much in life from this couple, both sweet lessons and bitter ones. The sacrifice they gave in leaving western comforts and coming to West Africa, a vastly different culture than they were accustomed to, spoke of their sincerity.

Devotion to missions was a life calling for the missionary couple and one they embraced very seriously. However, it became evident that it was a difficult thing for them to fully embrace the new culture and people without holding strongly, though perhaps unwittingly, to ingrained biases. Cultural and racial prejudices came through. As these prejudices displayed themselves it was very painful for us, we did not understand how one minute we could feel their love for us and the next be made to feel so small and insignificant. It was hard to face the attitudes, actions, and comments that would periodically erupt which spoke to us of anything but love and acceptance.

As young men, we felt the sting of being seen merely as the 'African boys, merely helping to assist the prominent foreigners accomplish their mighty mission goals to lost Africa. We reminded ourselves during especially challenging times, that the best choice was to hold our ground of joy in Jesus. We determined that no matter what, our aim would be to do everything not for man's acceptance but rather, "As unto the Lord."

During the eight years of container living, the missionary man would often promise that the church building was going to include a new home for us. This was easy to grasp as there were many buildings going up all over the church's compound, and we took heart in knowing that one of them would soon be our home. We were so excited, and relied on his words of promise.

After eight years the building projects were nearing completion. It was then we learned with no prior discussion or notice, that the missionary had sold the metal shipping container we were living in. Out of the blue he came and told us that our home of all those years would be gone within a few days and we would have to find other places to live. No mention of the promised home at the church property was made at this time or ever after. The suddenness of the information, and curtness with which it was relayed to us, was extremely difficult to take. There was no time to really prepare ourselves or process anything. All we could do was pack up and leave.

I had embraced this missionary man and his wife as family, I still felt love for them and perhaps this is why it hurt me so much to see that my own feelings seemed of little value. In many ways my brothers and I had opened our hearts in trust towards them. I went into the bathhouse that afternoon and sat on the cold stone slab of the shower. Tears streamed down my face as I struggled to understand. Confusing and unanswered questions tumbled through my mind. *Why couldn't he have discussed this with us sooner? Do we not count for anything more than a few days notice? How can he sell our home right out from underneath? What are we going to do now? Where will I live?*

It wasn't so much about the loss of the container home, or the dispersion that would surely come as we frantically searched for new places to stay, no, my pain arose from a deeper place. The old wounds of rejection ripped open once again.

As the missionary had declared so it played out. Our container was removed quickly and we all scrambled to find shelter elsewhere. I did not have family or relatives to return to as some of the others did, but God was looking out for me. A tent immediately became my new house. It may not have been much, but it was a place to sleep and stay dry for which I was grateful.

A new missionary family arrived around this time. They were quite a bit younger than the first missionaries and very ready to take up the reigns of the mission, even as the first missionary couple had decided to return to the USA. In addition to electrical work I soon became very involved with these new missionaries as they needed an interpreter, driver and help with navigating this new culture and country. I found myself traveling with them to the northern part of Ghana to help with mission outreaches. Visiting groups from America would often come for short stints of time and we would take them to new places in the north to spread the gospel.

Unfortunately, it soon became clear that the new missionaries were more racially insensitive than the first missionaries. This time of my life became extremely difficult. It quickly became evident to me that I had value to them, but little worth in their eyes.

One day I overheard the missionary talking to a visiting volunteer, "Michael, he has the skill to draw the crowds but sure doesn't have the brains to teach them anything." While not spoken directly to my face, these words cut deep. I knew in my heart that God had destiny for my life and I pressed in closer to hear His words of truth in the midst of conflicting voices. Time and again I had to run to Papa God and give Him my hurt feelings. Jesus was my example to follow. He suffered so much more than I ever could, and this was at the hands of those He loved. Because of His grace I could also choose to extend forgiveness to the ones who hurt me.

While this season of my life was not easy, it certainly wasn't all hurt and pain. There was a lasting blessing that God brought my way in that I met many nice foreigners who came to also help and work with the missionary family. So many of these short term visitors were completely the picture of Jesus' love to me and some of them have remained lifelong friends. I thank God so much for each individual who did not allow the stark differences of culture, class and color to become a stumbling block of disaster and cruelty. These loving ones came along sometimes for only a few short weeks at a time, but they came with such a genuine love and openness. I felt truly valued by so many of them. They will never know to what degree the impact of their friendship influenced my life. It truly helped me to release the deep hurts that others helped create.

1 Peter 4.8 has an amazing verse that reads, "Love covers a multitude of sin!" And it is so true. To live in an environment that was relentlessly attacking my identity and worth was not easy. I so naturally could have, at this point, embraced a life entrenched in victimhood, bitterness and hatred. But Jesus had shown me a different path to follow and so I made an intentional choice to love instead of hate. I looked away from broken humans and focused my

74

eyes steadfastly towards the One who is Love Himself. I know that the Holy Spirit genuinely helped me to love others well. And with my choice to love, God supernaturally charged my heart with His joy. There was such a joy in my heart that no outside human or circumstance could extinguish it.

## Adopted

One memorable day I happened to meet a man by the name of Andrew. He was visiting the mission house when we were introduced. Upon greeting Andrew that day I quickly warmed to this man's kind and happy spirit that shone out to those around him. I came to learn that Andrew was also a missionary to Ghana and had recently arrived in Kumasi along with his wife and two young children. As they were setting up home in the city and navigating the ropes of a new language and culture, God began to intersect our paths and a friendship between the two of us began to grow. Early on after their arrival some of the electrical fixtures in Andrew's home broke, or perhaps, they were never working in the first place. When he learned of my electrical abilities Andrew approached the missionary I had been helping, to see if he could ask me to come and fix the problems for his family.

Always eager for work and somewhat curious to meet my new friend's family I arrived, tools in hand, at their gate early in the morning. I stopped only momentarily before knocking boldly. I was soon ushered into their simple home. It did not take long to fix a broken fan among other things, and when everyone arrived home later in the day they were delighted to find the room much cooler than before.

The missionaries' two small children, Lucas and Luiza, were delightful from the very start. Before I left that first day I had gained the friendship of two of the cutest and smallest missionaries I'd ever seen. Their squeals of joy and laughter lingered in my ears as I smiled all the way back down the street that evening. It had been a wonderful day.

After fixing the fan, it wasn't long before my new friends approached me about the possibility of moving into their gatehouse. My first thoughts were, *I live in a tent! Do they even know how much of a blessing it would be to move into a solid room?* My heart was flowing with gratitude. This sudden unexpected offer caught me completely by surprise.

A gatehouse is a small building located right by the front gate of many of the newer city homes in Ghana. It is used as the office for a security guard to stay in while he watches over the main house. A shelter from the common downpours of rain, and a shade from the sweltering sun. I happily accepted the offer and soon had packed away my tent for good and gathered up what few possessions I owned, more than ready to move into my very own gatehouse.

It was a small room hardly big enough to call a bedroom. For me it was perfect. During the night I became a watchman over their compound. In the morning I would be on the way to attend to electrical jobs in town. I loved the rhythm of my new circumstance. Living as part of this family quickly developed a very close bond between us. I endearingly referred to them as Mom and Dad, although they were not too much older than I. For so long I had desired to experience life within a true christian family and I finally found myself immersed in a dream come true.

Juliana, or Mom, was tremendously knowledgeable as a pediatric doctor; she was such a loving mother to her children and devoted wife towards Andrew. Mom was always willing to share encouragement and wisdom with me. Andrew came alongside me as a father like no one had ever done before and poured into my life his love, friendship and wise counsel. As for the children they were the epitome of joy and hope in action. I loved my newest little brother and sister with all my heart and delighted in their simple faith and great happiness.

Both Mom and Dad spared nothing in teaching me about God's Kingdom of love. However it didn't stop there, for they also practically showed me God's love in a multitude of tangible ways. Both of them were very patient with me as I navigated all sorts of things, all the way from learning to drive a vehicle, ride a bicycle, to how a true gentleman treats a lady.

I cannot go further without mentioning another very dear member of the family, Vovo. Vovo was Juliana's mother, Grandma to us all, and while she did not live in Ghana she often visited with her family from her home in Brazil. She was perhaps one of the sweetest and most generous mamas I'd ever met. Her care for family was only rivaled by her love for God. What this family believed inwardly was almost always the way they lived outwardly. I was swept up in the blessing of it all.

## Lake Bosomtwe

One day Dad and Mom told me that their time in Kumasi was soon to finish as they had accepted a long term missions position at Amakom, a small village by the shores of Lake Bosomtwe. Lake Bosomtwe is about five miles across and interestingly, Ghana's only natural lake. Some speculate the lake is the result of a historic crater carved out suddenly by a violent meteorite collision. The lake is surrounded by lush forests and twenty four small and isolated villages.

I was overjoyed when they asked me if I would consider joining them in the mission at the lake. Of course this would mean giving up my current work as an electrician but I had no hesitation in my spirit and quickly agreed to move with them. It was to be a missions adventure for all of us and soon began in full as we packed up and journeyed out of Kumasi and up into the hill country.

Once settled at the lake, the days slipped swiftly into weeks and then months. There was much to be involved with. Life and ministry quickly consumed our time. It was very draining physically at times and yet constantly rewarding to see God's hand move in this little corner of Ghana. I enjoyed having my own house at the compound. It sat high on the hill overlooking the large lake. Taking my trumpet I loved to sit on the porch and blast notes of worship as far as my lungs could send them. It was a joyful noise graciously accepted by most and escaped by none.

How full the days were from dawn to dark. Sometimes it was translating, at other times preaching or traveling to buy supplies in the city. We also hosted teams of short term missionaries. Often we were involved in visiting the neighboring villages around the lake which we primarily traveled to by way of small boats. Whatever we found ourselves doing one thing was certain, there was never a dull moment.

Around this time Mom and Dad helped me in the purchase of a plot of land for a future home. It was a fair drive down the mountain from the lake where we lived and securely nestled on a small rise overlooking an expanse of bushland. A talented friend of mine generously drew up an expansive house plan and as able I slowly began to purchase bricks and set them in place for this future home.

The lake ministry was touching many lives when out of the blue a devastating and deadly cholera outbreak swept into the region. It quickly went through village after village around the lake. The small clinic, desperately in need of an upgrade, instantly became the hub of earnest activity as many sick people flooded in for help. The dire situation begged all our focus, energy and attention. It wasn't easy and so with prayers, tears, sweat and sleepless nights we forged ahead in the strength that God gave us. With thankful hearts we finally saw an end to this tragic epidemic.

Thankfully alongside the hardships came big blessings in tiny packages. Nothing caused more joy than the arrival of new babies being born at the clinic. These little lives were a constant reminder that our God was creating new life, new hope, and new destinies. Even Andrew and Juliana's third son was miraculously born on a rain soaked, glorious night far from modern amenities.

All these things and more were the making of memories that would last a lifetime. No amount of witchcraft, of which there was an abundance, could discourage us from our passion of seeing Jesus break through in our lives and the lives of those around us. Heaven covered us in the protecting blood of Jesus as our prayers, praise and practical demonstrations of the love of Christ resounded in that lake region.

# Chapter 9 - Across the Continent

**"And now, just as you accepted Christ Jesus as your Lord,
you must continue to follow Him.
Let your roots grow down into Him, and let your lives be built on Him.
Then your faith will grow strong in the truth you were taught,
and you will overflow with thankfulness.
~ Colossians 2:6-7 NLT ~**

"**Y**ou've got to read these!" Dad said as he pushed yet another fascinating looking book across the table in my direction. The look on his face reflected Mom's joyful expression as she smiled at us from above her pile of clean laundry. I knew that something incredible must have taken place for them to return from their furlough in America with all these books. Books are heavy items to travel anywhere with let alone across the world, especially considering the strict luggage limitations. The books obviously were treasures and I was eager to take a closer look and a deeper read of them. As I looked intriguingly at the covers, Dad explained how one of the authors, a woman by the name of Heidi Baker and her husband Rolland, had started a mission far away in an east African country. "There is a mighty move of God and a mission school there. I wish we could go if only it were possible." He dreamed aloud, eyeing again the pile of colorful books. "I'll go for you!" I volunteered with a laugh. Dad smiled and laughed along with me, "Well, you'd better get to reading so you know where you're headed then."

The books were so inspiring and compelling I soon became lost in all the stories, testimonies and revelations. In fact, I had completely forgotten my offer to go to the mission school when Dad called me aside a few weeks later and posed the following question. "Would you like to travel?" he asked one afternoon. I was blown away. Did he just ask me if I wanted to travel? "Yes, of course I want to travel!" I replied. I had been praying about what my future was to look like. Now, in my mind's eye I pictured the continent of Africa, disappearing from view even as the comforts of the western world emerged on my glorious imagined horizon of ease and opportunity.

Growing up in Ghana the only picture of the west I had been given was what few scenes came through in magazine articles and dusty television screens. The west looked like a perfect place with no poverty or trouble, just magnificent homes and massive amounts of material things that seemed to make all who owned them very happy. This was quite the misconception, but at that time I had no other grid for the reality of what the west was like. Who wouldn't want to visit such an extravagant place?

**"Where am I going?"**

In my excitement and hearty agreement to travel, the one small detail I forgot to ask was, 'where am I going?' When Dad started to explain the details of this journey my wide grin wilted like a picked flower in the hot sun. Listening closely I learned that I was not going west but rather east to Mozambique. Mozambique? This African country was full of extreme poverty and disease. I was shocked. I didn't like the thought of life becoming even more difficult. What kind of a vacation would that be anyway? It was especially shocking since I had happily been envisioning something altogether different.

Thankfully, any initial dismay was only short lived. My hopes rose up again upon hearing Dad reassure me that it wasn't a mistake. God had abundantly provided the means and I had already been accepted to attend the mission school run by missionaries Heidi and Rolland Baker. My mind soon was zipping

81

back through the books I had recently read from this couple. I was reminded of how, instead of clinging to their comfortable life, the Baker's had left the west in order to move to Mozambique, all because it was the poorest nation.

They had an amazing passion for God and compassion for people. What an inspiration this was to me! The children's homes they started, miraculous testimonies of daily miracles and an ever increasing number of vibrant churches springing up all pointed to the fact that a glorious work of God was indeed underway in this nation. Quickly the smallest of anxieties inside me were replaced with a growing excitement about the journey ahead. I was hungry for more of God. Mozambique was the place God was leading me to.

**Mozambique school of missions**

I could barely believe it when the day of departure arrived and the stewardess asked us to buckle our seat belts for takeoff. I was on my way to Mozambique. Cinching my belt tightly, I hung on even more as the plane sped down the runway and lifted off the tarmac. I had always felt that the ground beneath my feet was stable. As the plane that day left the ground my sense of stability left me. So far up there in the sky I knew there was nothing solid under my feet. What tree could I cling to for support if this plane decided to come down? Thankfully, the question never had to be answered as God's grace was sufficient and I survived my first plane ride. We arrived safely in Pemba, Mozambique, East Africa.

Once at the children's home, I met so many new people in such a short time. It was amazing to try and take in all the different personalities and outlooks. Almost all the mission students had traveled from the United States and Europe and so the coming weeks were to give plenty of opportunities to experience life in a maze of diverse culture. I was eager to experience all God had for us.

Throughout the school my heart was touched many times by God for the world around me. A desire to see God's Kingdom expand throughout the world grew.

As students we would sit on the ground listening to ministry leaders from all around the world who came to share with us the great things God was doing in their respective regions. Their simple yet profound teachings were inspiring and encouraging.

As one of the first African nationals to attend this mission school, I found myself sometimes mistaken for a local. Once we were riding in the back of a truck to an outreach location when the police pulled us over and demanded to see everyone's visa. One by one my western classmates dug through their bags and pulled out the required documents. When my turn came the policeman addressed me in the national language of Portuguese. I couldn't understand a word he was saying. Nevertheless, I had learned one sentence in Portuguese and so I used it with confidence, "Sorry, I don't speak Portuguese." I said. The policeman looked at me and in English replied, "What do you mean you don't speak Portuguese?" Promptly he bypassed me and asked the next classmate for their documents.

The villages we would go to on outreaches were filled with many desperate people. Even in their poverty they were hungry for God, I was undone to see this kind of hunger and forever changed by the love God showed in these primitive places. I was challenged in my own walk with God to steward well all that He had placed in my own life.

My favorite memories of Mozambique are most certainly of the children, both at the mission base, which was home to a few hundred children, and in the surrounding areas. Getting to know them and spending time sowing joy into each life day by day was an incredible blessing. To see the little ones' smiles get even bigger over the smallest meal we shared together, prayer that was prayed or the simplest game played was better than anything else. I feel that God really placed such a love in my heart for each child I met in Mozambique. Most of them were a bundle of exuberant energy, while others were quite solemnly gripped with their realities of difficulty and lack, and of course, a few were altogether naughty. Across the spectrum of little people I was often reminded of my own childhood not so long ago and how God loved me and cared for me in my own corner of the world even when I didn't know who He was. God loves us no matter who we are or where we live. The obstacles we have to face are all mere stepping stones for the God who created us and loves us more than we'll ever comprehend. I prayed for the children, played with them and encouraged them as often as I could.

**"Where is the Doctor?"**

While in Mozambique I became friends with a christian young man who lived in the community outside the children's home. One day during a class session I noticed my friend frantically waving, beckoning me to come quickly. I slipped out from under the open thatched roof classroom and hurried towards my Mozambican brother. "What is going on?" I asked him. "My sister in law is in serious trouble. Please, you have to come quickly to pray for her!" He begged me. He went on to say that his sister in law had been in labor for many hours, but the baby was not coming out. The emergency operation she was in need of had been canceled because the family did not have money to pay for the procedure. I could hardly believe that the desperate woman was discharged right out of the door of a hospital, and if that wasn't shocking enough the doctor himself had already left for home. "How is this possible?" I thought – "Especially in a life and death situation! It is such a small amount of money needed, I even have the money in my pocket." There was no time for pondering questions as the two of us hurried to the main road and soon were on the back of a motorcycle making our way as fast as possible towards the hospital.

Finally we arrived at the facility and came across a very upsetting sight. My friend's sister in law lay thrashing on the ground right outside the front entrance. Her entire body was covered in dust and sweat from all the turmoil she was going through. It was clearly evident that the lady and her unborn child were in a very serious condition. Without intervention they were dying right there in the dirt. Her family stood helplessly nearby, worry evident on every face.

Rushing past the family I quickly found one of the nurses. "Where is this woman's doctor?" I asked with urgency. The nurse looked up from her work and responded, "Oh, he already left. The money is not enough for him to be able to help her." Not wasting a second I said to the nurse, "Call him to come back then! The cost is covered." She nodded her head and reached for the phone. Leaving the nurse I went straight back outside to the laboring woman and started to pray.

Time was not on the woman's side, but God was on her side. *Nothing is impossible with You Lord, You have said this in Your word.* In that critical moment thoughts of God's faithfulness began to burn in my heart and my spirit reached out to grasp the faith He alone could give that was needed for this very desperate situation. *You are good God, full of compassion.* Kneeling on the dirt beside the ailing woman, I placed a hand on her shoulder and began crying out to God for a merciful miracle. I don't know how long I prayed this way, I was so passionate to see God rescue and save this woman and her unborn child. The family also joined in and together our voices rose in earnest prayer to God. We only stopped when it was told to us that the doctor was arriving at the hospital. As the woman was admitted once more, I handed my friend the necessary money for surgery, advising him to hold onto the money for after the baby was born. "I believe the Lord is already answering our prayers and there will be no need for a surgery today." I felt a settling peace in my spirit as I left the hospital and made my way back to the school.

It was later that very same day that my friend came once again to find me. This time he was not frantic with concern but rather bursting with joy to share the good news that the baby had been safely delivered and no surgery was needed. A miracle, praise God! A while later, when the family was home from the hospital I went with a classmate to visit them and greet this miracle baby. It was such a wonderful moment to witness the goodness of God. Both the mother and her baby were alive and healthy. I was delighted upon learning that she had named her baby boy Michael. Together we all praised God for such a miraculous gift of life and the mercies of God's loving care.

**Return to the Lake**

My time in Mozambique quickly came to an end. My life had changed much over the last few months and I felt such a fresh, vibrant desire in my heart for God and His Kingdom. With a multitude of memories tucked away and a hope for the purposes of God ahead, I climbed aboard the aircraft that would take me back home to Ghana. Sooner than I could imagine I found myself right back on the familiar shores of Lake Bosomtwe.

Hardly had I arrived back to the mission house at the lake and unpacked my bags when the winds of change began to swirl around our compound. My dearly loved family found themselves caught up in the unexpected reality of having to leave the country of Ghana and return to their home country of Brazil as quickly as possible. I will always remember this turbulent time and yet, while I could understand that life is ever changing, and perhaps, change is the only constant in life, I was still devastated to have to have to say goodbye. It all came so suddenly there was no time for any of us to adequately prepare for this transition. My family from afar had come close enough to completely adopt me into their hearts as a son and a friend. How those few short years with them had flown by. Our friendships had blossomed like a vibrant rose and yet on that day of final goodbyes all I could feel were sharp thorns.

Especially during this time I clung to God in prayer, knowing that He alone would sustain me day by day. He was the fire that burned in my heart and the One who promised to never leave. On the day of their departure it was very hard for us all. There were more tears than anyone of us wanted to shed in a day. Drained and sorrowful I returned to the lake alone, I sat down on the patio of my little lake house as the evening approached. I let out a long sigh. Everything around me seemed to sit so still and lonely. It was hard to look on the sloping hill below and see the empty mission house so recently filled with the ones I loved. Their absence was tangible. Usually by this time of day the air would be filled with the interesting smells of their foreign food, mixing like harmony with the musical sounds of their equally foreign accents.

Baby banter, child laughter, it was all there so close in my memory and yet so awkwardly far away in the present. I sat on the step and closed my eyes, lost in thoughts and memories.

"Hi Michael!" The voice called. "Hi!" I replied, quickly opening my eyes just in time to see a passing village friend on the road below. The dust of his sandals seemed to propel the man right out of sight for he disappeared behind the clinic quickly. Although the clinic had been open and functional there was still a lot of work to be done on the building. Before Andrew and his family had left I gave them my promise that I would stay for the completion of the clinic. Regardless of the many unknowns ahead I was willing to remain at the lake for them and to help them realize their dream.

The following months were hard as challenges cropped up in many places and on many fronts. And yet, with each challenge came the faithfulness of God to bring a solution. Time and again I knew He was strengthening me in faith, endurance and character. Keeping close to Papa God in prayer was vital and sustained my life helping to keep me strong in the joy that His Presence brought.

During this time, there were those around me who would often advise me to take and put aside for myself some of the building funds that came from overseas. "You're the one helping complete this construction, they'll never know if you take some of the cash, and besides, you have your own future and house to think about. You deserve at least a little more for your efforts. I'm sure they would gladly have you take a little." These small temptations would be said in all earnestness. Sadly, it was a surprisingly common sentiment given to me by pastors and fellow Christians alike. Call it whatever and justify the action however one did, I knew this would be stealing and I refused to steal. Whatever the cost could be to my own future endeavors God was my provider, I would not compromise even a coin. Instead, I put my thoughts and energy to see that the clinic went forward to completion.

As for my own home's construction there simply wasn't the time or the funding to continue. Being away in Mozambique and then putting all efforts towards the completion of the clinic the construction of my own home quickly came to a standstill. The fast growing African bush quickly enveloped the foundation blocks that had been laid and grass grew so tall all around my home. All that could be seen was one large pile of unused blocks waiting for progress to resume. Unfortunately this delay did not go unnoticed. One day a pastor living nearby saw that my house had stopped getting bigger. He decided to "borrow" the entire large pile of unused blocks I had piled carefully beside my house and use them for his own construction. When I finally was able to make a visit to my land I saw that my blocks were missing. Asking around the small community it did not take long to find the guilty culprit. The pastor made no delay in quite openly admitting to the 'borrowing' of my blocks. Try as I did, I couldn't understand how one can borrow blocks, especially seeing that they were now solidly set into the walls of his own home. The pastor apologized profusely and we soon came to a mutual agreement that the blocks would be traded for water from his well. The water would be very useful to me for the continued construction of my home, whenever that time arrived.

Many months and much effort later the clinic was finally completed. It had been a lonely uphill battle for me with not much local support and a lot of resistance coming from denominational leadership in the bigger city. I set a time and spread the word for the opening ceremony of the clinic's completion. However, on the decided day we agreed for, other than some of the locals, nobody showed up. I stood there waiting for the church leaders and officials to arrive. Finally as the hours ticked by the locals quietly slipped back to their homes for the evening. I realized with a sigh of sadness that nobody was coming to acknowledge anything. I ended up having to gently lay the new keys on the front step of the clinic for the church leaders to find whenever they decided to come. While there remained no recognition as to the clinic's completion, I for one was very glad to have the clinic completed. It was ready for full service to the communities around the lake. The locals were delighted. This fact brought me happiness.

Leaving the lake, I moved back to Kumasi. Gladly I accepted the offer of a small office to live in. It was at the same church I had helped clear the land for so many years ago. Not wanting to sit around waiting for life to happen, I quickly became as useful as I could at the church and found myself busier than ever. Between electrical repair around the compound, washing the pastors cars, leading out in prayers, going on visitation with the associate pastor, running errands, teaching Sunday School, keeping the generator in good working condition and any other such maintenance work at the church that came my way I stayed very busy. Often I was pulled in many directions, by many people.

God really provided for me during that interim season. I am so grateful for each kind individual who stepped in to give encouragement and support to me. As the days passed, and my time was spent attending to the simple tasks of day to day life around the church, I constantly kept an eye on the horizon of my life. I felt deeply in my spirit that God had a specific destiny for me to fulfill. I sensed that faithfulness in the ordinary work that filled each day, was essential to future success. God indeed was about to open a very big door in my life - leading me to countries, experiences, miracles, and people I had never dreamed of.

# Chapter 10 - An Ocean of Possibility

"If I take the wings of the morning
and dwell in the uttermost parts of the sea,
even there Your hand shall lead me, and Your right hand shall hold me."
~ Psalm 139:9-10 ~

S prawled out along the tropical coastline of Ghana sits the country's capital city of Accra. This city is a metropolis of extreme proportions. Centuries old African culture is embedded right alongside the fast pace of a modern life, increasingly changing and expanding the face of the city. Friends living in Accra were in need of some electrical work to be done in their house and I was always eager for an adventure outside the bounds of Kumasi. I had been to Accra before but the city still made me shake my head in amazement. I was happy to visit and be of help to my friends. While at their home this couple shared with me about a very interesting ministry. My curiosity grew with excitement as they told me about a certain ship named the Africa Mercy which sailed along the west coast of Africa. It was a christian hospital ship, providing free medical services to many people in the countries that sit along the West African coastline. When I learned that there was an opening for a volunteer deckhand my excitement grew. I called my family in Brazil to share with them the fascinating idea of joining the ship. They were such an encouragement and help in making this possibility a reality. With much prayer and joy I had soon applied and been accepted. I was on my way to sea.

I never dreamed of working onboard a ship. I had no experience on the water other than moving some small boats around on Lake Bosomtwe. Lack of knowledge however was not a hindrance as God opened wide this brand new door. December 2010, a few months after my 31st birthday, I said goodbyes in Kumasi and boarded a plane to South Africa ready to meet and join the team of the Africa Mercy ship. A lot of encouragement from loved ones in Brazil spurred me on to take up the challenge of learning the skills needed to be a good deckhand. I first went to a set time of training in Durban, South Africa.

**Launched into the deep**

"Okay, now what we are going to do next is jump right off the ship and swim back to the dock." our instructor said with finality as he doled out life vests and pointed, far too nonchalantly, towards the ship's high railing. Laughter erupted as many of the guys strode their way bravely to the jump. I on the other hand gulped, "Is he serious?" I could already feel my knees begin to buckle at the very thought of jumping in that water. Trailing behind my peers, I crept towards the railing and peered down, down, down to the murky water below.

During the previous day's class we had been shown a film about creatures of the sea, not even one of them looked like anything I would want to meet. And yet now, as I gazed across the salty water below all I could envision were these creatures swimming just beneath the surface, ready and waiting to meet and eat me. I shuddered at the thought. "Michael, you're up next!" the instructor said with what sounded to me like far too much eagerness in his voice. I responded weakly with, "Ahh, actually I don't think... well, can I postpone this jump?" With a faint smile of amusement my instructor boomed, "Not at all Michael, this is the jump and this is the day. After all man, it's required to complete your training. You've got to do it and I know you can." There was no backing out, turning around, or trailing off and so I went ahead and jumped in. The salty splash soon gave way to relieved laughter as I crawled out of the water a short time later. I was grateful to survive just like everyone else and together we finished our training all prepped for life at sea.

During the days leading up to our 18 day sail to Sierra Leone, the ship was a bustle of activity. Many crew members continued to arrive and settle into the little snug cabins. There was a tremendous amount of work that went into preparing the entire hospital ship for a voyage through the unknown terrain of shifting ocean waves. Many busy hands pitched in to cover, close, tie down and secure everything. From the surgical tables and instruments in the hospital to the pots, pans and food in the galley, every last moveable item in the ship had to be stored, secured and prepared for the chance of rough seas. Excitement was tangible and increasing as groups of crew went up and down the gangway in little huddles those last few days. Whether to buy personal supplies, meet with friends, or simply enjoy that soon to be missing feeling of stable turf. I watched with awe as the large crane atop the ship hoisted each land-rover, and there were plenty of them, onto the top of the ship. Once unloosed the mechanic then tied each vehicle down onto the deck with large straps and chains.

With around 300 crew onboard, as the day of departure drew near I could hardly believe there could be so many unfamiliar faces in such a small place. One day as I sat at a table in the dining hall with two other deckhands, a curly haired girl wearing a flour covered baseball hat and soiled galley apron came and sat down at the empty seat. She smiled and introduced herself to us as Bobbi. "What is your name?" She asked me. I told her my name and listened as she asked more questions. "Where are you from?" "What do you do?" When she asked, "How did you get here?" I couldn't help but laugh out loud. It certainly seemed to me that the more westerners I met the more convinced I was becoming that they all loved to talk and talk. She was still waiting for a response so I said, "Prayer." Amusingly this simple answer didn't satisfy Bobbi at all, she went right on to ask, "So, prayer? What do you mean by that?" I laughed again and kept it simple "Prayer. God brought me here." She smiled at me, clearly seeing that my response was lacking vastly in detail and then thankfully she turned her attention to eating lunch.

Soon after that we became casual friends. Even though she asked lots of questions Bobbi was still quite reserved compared to others. I liked her as a friend but that was as far as it went for me. I really felt that God was saying no to any serious relationship at this time. While she never said or did anything flirtatious, there remained something stirring in me of which I couldn't quite describe that made me feel it necessary to address our friendship in clear terms. I sat her down one day and told her straight, "Bobbi I need to tell you something. God has called me and I have dedicated my life to missions. If my shirt pocket represented my life there's only room in it for Jesus, God and Holy Spirit but there is no room for you." I wasn't upset and certainly not intending to hurt my friend. But from the shocked look that flashed across her face I could see that Bobbi obviously hadn't been expecting such direct talk and certainly didn't intend on being in my pocket herself. She was very kind though and we remained friends after this. I was glad for that.

**Life at Sea**

Pulling on my boots I laced them tightly before pushing open the heavy berth door and stepping out into the long hallway of deck four. Climbing up the stairs and hallways through the decks I emerged out onto the open deck of the ship's port side. It was a beautiful evening and I was grateful to be starting my shift in time to enjoy the setting sun as it spilled it's last rays of warmth and fiery colors over the expanse of water. The ocean was calm tonight and the ship gently swayed this way and that in relaxing motion as we moved steadily ahead. Soon I was reporting in with the deckhand coming off his shift. "You're on tonight brother, keep a good watch out for those pirates." he cautioned me. We were currently sailing past a country that is known for it's dangerous pirate activity. These modern day pirates are notorious for coming up around larger ships on their small speed boats and attempting to break in to steal, wreck havoc, or worse. I nodded, noting the seriousness of my duty.

Nighttime felt much like daytime for me, especially after years of cultivating the night hours of my life with prayer, staying awake at night was not difficult.

Now the nights were filled with the added responsibility of being the best eyes and ears I could be, ready to spot and alert of any potential trouble. While most of the crew dreamed and snored contentedly on their swaying cots, I walked the decks that night and scanned the dark waves, praying and worshiping as I went. Thankfully, we never encountered trouble on our voyage to Sierra Leone. After 18 days at sea we safely entered the port of Devastation Bay, Sierra Leone, in the early months of 2011.

**Sierra Leone**

We were a busy hospital ship in a desperate nation. Even in dock there were always responsibilities that demanded attention. I continued to spend many of the long night hours in prayer and worship as I patrolled the ship decks. Now that we were docked, working shifts at night meant the day was free and I could leave the ship. God's grace alone was strengthening me because often after a long night shift I would rest just a little or bypass sleep altogether and head into town instead. One of my favorite things to do was go into the city of Freetown to find new friends and share the gospel of Jesus. I thank God that He introduced me to a lot of people who were receptive to hear about Jesus. It did not matter to me whether I ministered on the ship, traveled to a distant location, or took a local trip to a nearby market or beach, I was eager to engage with my brothers and sisters in this war torn and poverty stricken land. I wanted them to experience the same river of God's love that welled up inside of me. As the weeks went by God opened incredible doors of favor as I moved with Him.

**Deliverance At Devil's Hole**

"Please don't go Michael, it's not safe at all!" cautioned yet another well intention-ed friend as I passed through the ship's reception one day. "You know Michael, that really isn't the place to try and evangelize." another concerned individual added in the hopes of changing my plans. I had been asked by a local pastor, and agreed, to join him in a small crusade in one of the rough areas of Freetown. The name of the place, Devil's Hole, gave evidence to how even the locals viewed this spot. Not only was it surrounded by families living in abject poverty and addictions, but the land itself was known for it's dark history of disaster. Crime, accidents and death were continually being recorded. The amount of blood that had spilled in this place only gave way to demonic activity all the more. Witchcraft was rampant and violence evident.

I was not naive to the realities governing this place, and certainly I was not about to go where God did not lead me; However, as I prayed for direction I strongly felt Him calling me to join the pastor and minister to the souls of Devil's Hole. Were they not in need of God's love just like the rest of us? God had not given me a spirit of fear so I simply could not partner with others fearful concerns. In preparing to leave the ship for the evening's crusade, I was stopped in the hall by a fellow Ghanaian friend, "Michael I know you're going out tonight, I would like to pray for you." She offered. I happily obliged as she prayed over me for great breakthroughs and the Lord's protection. God was about to answer these prayers in a dramatic way. I thanked her heartily as I waved goodbye and walked down the gangway.

Once off the ship, I was going alone so had to find my own way to the ministry location. I waved down a motorcyclist taxi and climbed onto the seat behind the rider. Soon we were moving through the intensely busy streets of the city. As we neared Devil's Hole, my eyes opened wide in horror to see a car hurtling right towards us at a very great speed. As it got closer I could see that the driver was out of control and definitely going to crash right into my leg. The motorbike driver was doing all he could to turn out of the way but there was a deep ditch to his side and nowhere else to go. The motorbike had a small chance of clearing the car but with no extra inch to spare my leg would most surely catch the full impact of the oncoming vehicle. There was absolutely nothing I could do to prevent this serious accident. All I could do was cry out to Jesus, and at that very instant I felt a strong hand grip my shoulder and pull me swiftly up, clean off the back of the bike. Before I realized what had happened I found myself standing safely on the curbside without so much as a scratch. My driver had stopped the motorbike. He was wiping the sweat of concern off his forehead and breathing heavily after such a near miss. He looked back at me in shock, "How on earth did you get way over there? Did you jump from my bike?" He gasped. "No, I could not even jump," I replied equally amazed, "God miraculously delivered me today!"

With grateful hearts we continued on our way and made it safely to the crusade. God flooded Devil's Hole with His Presence that night. Many souls were touched, healed and delivered as they experienced the love of Jesus for the first time and felt the darkness over their lives lifted by the power of Holy Spirit. I was so grateful to God for allowing me to partner with Him in loving those who were so often overlooked. The light of Jesus truly shone bright as Devil's Hole became filled to overflowing with Jesus' hope.

**Shout His name louder!**

I was leaving the ship one afternoon when I came across a very sick woman. She was just sitting outside the gate which led towards the ship. While there are many surgeries that the ship is equipped to help with, there are certain conditions that the ship simply is not equipped to accommodate. Due to the nature of this particular woman's sickness she was not able to go to the ship for treatment. But she was in a lot of pain. It was evident to all who could see her that her body was struggling a lot. Around this woman a small group of bystanders had gathered. As I approached them I could hear the pitiful woman crying out, "Allah, Allah, Allah!" and all the while Allah was not responding to her at all.

Bending down to her level I asked, "Mama, please can I pray for you?" "Oh, oh, oh the pain, go ahead!" She cried. And so I prayed and in doing so Jesus gave me an idea. Ideas from God are always worth acting on. Often it looks different in each situation, but God always has an idea, a strategy available and successful in our time of need. He is such a good Father. "Mama, Jesus wants to heal you." I said, "Please, will you shout the name of Jesus three times?

We'll see what He will do." The woman looked up at me, and even in her pain I could see that she wondered what kind of a request this was. All the same she complied though rather pitifully, "Jesus, Jesus..." The words were weak and hesitant. *God this declaration needs a jump start,* I thought. "Stop! Please wait a minute." I interrupted the woman before she had time to finish. The small group of bystanders was growing bigger and one simple glance assured me that most were not enthusiastic about the situation and all were skeptically curious. I continued, "Please mama, your voice is weak. I want you to say Jesus Name as if it is the most powerful Name you know, I want you to shout His name louder. Shout as loud as you can!"

Thankfully she was not offended at my intrusion and advice. But rather took a moment to weigh the cost and then all at once she did it. Taking a deep breath she shouted as loud as her lungs could expand. "JESUS!" The word erupted from her mouth with such a power she sprung clear off the ground and right onto her feet. Shocked is an understatement to describe the emotion this lady had as she looked down at herself. She was amazed. I was amazed. Those watching nearby were amazed to see her standing upright and pain free. The smile that came to her face that day as she described the miraculous healing coupled together with the joyful jumping as she began to dance was all glory to Jesus. He had healed her on the very same ground where so recently she sat with no hope. There was no denying to any of us the miracle Jesus had performed in her body.

"Therefore God has highly exalted Him, and given Him the name which is above every other name. That at the name of Jesus... every tongue should confess that Jesus is Lord, to the glory of God the Father." (Philippians 2.9-11)

**Prison Ministry**

While volunteering in Sierra Leone, God paved the way for me to begin going inside Freetown's prison. I stepped right into that prison door, and together with a fellow brother from the ship, we ministered to those inside. It was so special to be able to pray for the many inmates. I fondly remember the wonderful times spent encouraging those locked inside to trust in Jesus and give their lives to Him. Together with God's help we were able to bring much hope to those that were seeking something better for their lives. One day I told the group that had gathered to not give up on God, as miracles still happen in our day. "In fact," I said, "I believe very soon some of you will be miraculously released because of the grace of God over your lives."

Not too many days later I was walking in the busy marketplace when I heard the pounding of footsteps approaching from behind. An individual was shouting to get my attention, "Pastor Michael, pastor Michael!" I turned around to see where the voice was coming from and yet when I saw the man attached to the shouting I had no idea who he was. *How does he know me?* I wondered. The closer he got the happier he became until he closed in and wrapped me in a big hug. With unbounded joy he explained, "You may not even remember me, but I was in the prison that day when you spoke to us. You said that God was a God of miracles and He is! Look what He has done. I am out, because the Lord Jesus has set me free." I rejoiced with him and blessed him on his way.

I was totally happy to be able to minister in the prison, even though the conditions inside were quite despicable. I never dreamed that very close to where we ministered was an even darker, literally, and more dismal prison. God was going to open an opportunity to go there. It all started one afternoon when a prison guard asked me, "Michael, would you like to speak to the inmates at the condemned prison?" I was stunned at his invitation. I knew that condemned prisons do not allow visitors. The inmates in this facility are sentenced for life with no release. I could not begin to imagine what it would be like so I prayed for God to fill me up with wisdom and love. I'd never entered such a place in my life but with God leading I was so happy to follow. A day was arranged to enter and I made sure to arrive on the set day right on time.

I walked into the prison office and stopped short in surprise, it had clearly seen better days. An officer looked up from the depths of his dark seat and motioned for me to sit down. As he proceeded to check me in for the day, I had a good chance to look around the office. We weren't even in the prison and yet the office looked itself like a dungeon. Dust lay in thick sheets over everything in the room, even as mildew enveloped certain spots where the rain was seeping in from outside. Evidence of rats was everywhere. Their droppings piled across the floor and shelving. Every shelf held books containing prisoner records. The books themselves were a disaster. Most were terribly falling apart, all were rat gnawed and some were even damaged to the point of being completely illegible. The condition these books were in further reflected the hopeless plight of these men. I prayed again for the right words to encourage the condemned prisoners.

I thought the office was bad, but soon I realized it looked like a palace in comparison to the despair inside those locked prison doors. Once I stepped inside it was all I could do to avoid throwing up. I cannot even begin to describe the conditions inside that condemned prison. It was dreadful, smelled horrendous, and yet it was the prisoner's faces I will never forget. All around me was the stench and sight of misery, all covered in a thick atmosphere of utter hopelessness. I really thank God for filling my mouth with words that day, because honestly, in the natural it was very difficult to be there and witness fellow humanity in such deprivation. All of them were there because they had committed unimaginable atrocities, many were condemned to this place for the part they played in the tragic war. I stood there trying my best to not lose it totally. Like only He could have done Holy Spirit came close and put a love in my heart for those prisoners, by His supernatural grace I began to see the inmates as heaven must see all of us. So lost, and yet so valuable.

I don't recall much of what I said that day, but I do remember that I spoke about the hope that comes from knowing Jesus. I told them that Jesus condemns no individual who accepts the love and salvation He has for them. Whatever the circumstance of this world, a life that is given to God has forgiveness and the hope of an eternity in glory. Even within the very same place of confinement due to consequence here on earth, a life that finds itself in Jesus can experience joy that no person, place, or past history can take away. As I prayed for them so many tears were streaming down the faces around me, even my own. It was an incredible moment in time as Holy Spirit crashed into the depths of that despairing place and filled it with Jesus' light, love and eternal hope.

Like so many others who I met and prayed with in Sierra Leone, I was never privileged to meet the prisoners inside the condemned prison again. I don't know how many of them are still alive. I pray for those in that prison and trust that the Holy Spirit continued to water every seed that was sown in hearts that day. God promises us in Isaiah 55:1 "So shall My word be that goes forth from My mouth; It shall not return to Me void, But it shall accomplish what I please, And it shall prosper in the thing for which I sent it."

What an opportunity we have to shine the light of Jesus' love on those we meet along the way of life here on earth. We may never see them again this side of eternity but who knows if the love of God, which He gives us and we share is used by Him to become the defining moment for someone's salvation. Even if all you have to give is one small seed, and it seems to quickly disappear, keep praying for with God's watering it has the blessing and opportunity of growing and flourishing in His time.

# Chapter 11 - Into The Desert

"And we know that all things work together for good
to those who love God and are called according to His purpose."
~ Romans 8:28 ~

I hung up the phone one evening and immediately looked for the closest chair to sit in. I needed time to process this last conversation. Soon enough I found a quiet place and settled down to think about the future, the choices posed to me mere minutes ago ran as if on replay through my mind. Sitting there I could see through one of the ship's portal windows a local fishing boat as it headed for shore. I followed it with my eyes but my thoughts were far away pondering the invitation of my christian brother who I'd just been speaking with. He had asked if I would be open to coming to South Sudan to join him in building a school for one of the communities there. I must decide if I was going to leave the ship and accept this brother's adventurous offer or stay right here on board.

There were many aspects of life and ministry that I loved on the ship and I had made many good friends. God certainly brought me to the ship but was this season coming to a close? Was the invitation to South Sudan another mission He was bringing into my life? The more I spoke to my christian brother the more I began to anticipate all that could be accomplished if I were to go. This brother and I had met a few years previous in Mozambique. After that time he had traveled to South Sudan to do mission work and was now eagerly explaining how everything was ready to move forward on the school site, construction was waiting to begin as soon as I could arrive.

I prayed for quite some time before settling on the choice to leave the ship and fly to South Sudan. It was a major decision in my life and I did not leave without some around me who tried to convince me to stay. While I listened to their advice and cautions, I kept anticipating the future. Not only seeing my brother again, but also furthering the kingdom of God in this war torn and desperate nation. I knew there would be people along the way who could be introduced to Jesus and I knew that missions was a calling God had placed on my life. The last remaining tension holding me back seemed to be the cost it would take to fly across the continent of Africa. And so it was, when funds for a plane ticket to South Sudan were kindly donated by a very generous couple, I felt confident that I was on the right path.

As it turned out, this trip would become one of the most difficult times in my life. Often during this season it rang with clarity that I should have listened more closely to those who cautioned me against going. After receiving the money for my airline ticket, I had not waited for additional confirmation from God. Had I run ahead of Him too fast? Perhaps yes, but what I do understand now in looking back over this time is that God knows our hearts and motives. Even when we sometimes naively take a wrong turn, or the right turn too fast, or simply find ourselves on a troubling path outside of our control, God promises in Romans 8:28 to work all things for our good as we love Him.

In the stormy weeks ahead God stayed close by my side. I experienced God's protecting hand in my life time and again over those four months in ways I will never forget. He strengthened my heart, taught me great lessons in forgiveness, and challenged me to hold onto faith, hope and love even when all became so hard. It was also through this unusually difficult time, and in a very uncanny way, that God worked a wonderful good. As only He could have orchestrated, He brought me back into contact with a former friend, a young lady who would one day become my wife.

**"You're a Spy"**

My flight to South Sudan came via six different planes and layovers in a multitude of African nations. I was beyond exhausted when finally I reached the last touchdown in Uganda. From Kampala Airport the plan was to meet my brother who had invited me to join him and together we would take an overland trip north into the country of South Sudan. With a tired body and a spirit full of joy I walked off the plane and entered the customs area. After such a long journey I was so ready to rest and looking forward to a sound night's sleep.

I handed my passport to the customs officer and watched as he opened it. I wasn't paying too much attention until I noticed that instead of stamping and handing it straight back like those ahead of me, he stopped and studied it. All at once he ordered, "You wait right here." He stood up from his chair and swiftly walked away to show my passport to another officer. It was not encouraging to see a frown on his face when he returned. "Where are you going?" He demanded impatiently. I told him that I was on my way to South Sudan for missions. He looked me up and down, obviously not believing the answer I'd given. He continued incredulously, "White people go on missions, but you? You're an African and yet you say you're going on a mission?" I tried to reassure him that this was the truth. In a continued attempt to convince him I went on to say that I was meeting a friend, a white missionary friend, if that somehow made the difference. "He's coming to pick me up and take me to South Sudan." I said earnestly. "Prove it then." The officer snapped back.

What I thought would be simply pointing out my caucasian brother in the waiting area, turned out to be quite different. As I scanned the crowded room, not one white person could be seen anywhere. I began to sense the seriousness of the situation I faced. The custom's official was not impressed with my vain search for a white missionary but he did allow me to make a phone call. I called my brother and tried to explain my predicament. I was shocked to hear him say that he wasn't even close to the airport or even in the country of Uganda for that matter. "I sent you an email that I can't come Michael." he told me. I was shocked for I had not received any email prior to embarking on this journey. "What am I to do then?" I asked desperately, waiting for his answer. "I don't know." my friend replied matter of factly. He went on to explain, far too simply for the current situation, that I should just take a bus and make my own way north into South Sudan. He finished by assuring me that he'd meet me upon arrival there.

As the phone call disconnected I cried out to God in my heart, *What am I going to do now?* The customs officer snatched the phone and demanded to know when this white man was coming to pick me up. My case completely failed as I tried desperately to explain that I was indeed a missionary, but my friend was not coming to pick me up from the airport. "For the sake of God, please let me continue my journey." I pleaded. "For the sake of God, who's God? You're lying!" The officer exploded. "You're a spy, that's what! Now go sit down!" He slammed my passport into a locked box and called for another officer to come lock me up. As we went away I could hear the first officer jeeringly say, "African missionary, now that's a stretch."

The heavy door of the airport jail cell slammed behind me with a resounding clang. With no passport I had no identity. If escape was viable, which it was not, I still couldn't get back to Ghana, and I still couldn't go on towards South Sudan. In this crazy turn of events I was now a voiceless prisoner in Uganda, accused of being a spy and having nothing to prove otherwise. What was going on? My tired brain was trying to figure it all out, but I needed to sleep so I slid down the wall and sat on the cement floor.

Inside that small cell I was not alone, packed in like sardines were seven other people. Six men and one woman. When I tried to greet them, it quickly became evident that they all spoke Arabic and couldn't understand one word of my native tongue or English. The room had one small barred window and a fluorescent light glared over our heads constantly bright. Quickly our bodies heated the room up to a sweltering temperature and sweat was everywhere.

It almost goes without saying that the smell was terrible in that room. There was no air conditioning and no fan, just lots of mosquitoes.

I was locked in the airport jail for the next three days. I have no idea why the others were locked up but we were like family in a randomly unusual way. We tried to make the best of the grim situation, communicating with some improvised sign language. It wasn't long before they all became so desperate that they paid large bribes to the officers and were let free. I was told to pay a bribe too if I wanted to be released, but in addition to being innocent my funds were limited and I could not squander them on hefty bribes. Each day an officer was assigned to take me out to the market allowing me to buy some food to eat and go to the toilet. When I asked another officer on duty if there was anything that could be done to help my case he just looked at me with coldness and shrugged his shoulders. "No, nothing can be done for you." he said bluntly. It was a desperate situation, I was praying that God would deliver me somehow. It hadn't been that long ago that I was the one preaching to prisoners in Freetown and now here I was in the same locked up state. Didn't God miraculously release that guy who met me in the market? Nothing is impossible with Him and I knew God was able to work a miracle but I had to wait and trust. Thankfully, after three days God performed just such a miracle on my behalf.

Through His providential workings, a christian woman whose husband worked at the airport became aware of my plight. This woman whom I had never met talked with her husband, to see if maybe there was a chance he could speak a word to someone on my behalf. As only the Lord could have done, the woman's husband turned out to be the very same officer who curtly told me there was no hope. To God be the glory! After three trying days in the jail this same officer came and let me out. He realized the terrible mistake that had been made, and was very apologetic. By the grace of God, this officer not only opened my prison door but also took me in his personal car to the bus station. On the way to the station he stopped to buy me lunch as an added token of kindness. It was such a turn of favor in my dire circumstance, such a tangible miracle and

I was extremely grateful.

The bus finally brought me to the desired destination and landed me in the midst of South Sudan. I was so relieved to arrive and more than eager to join my brother and start building the school. After such positive phone calls between us, confirming that the foundation was in and building materials were waiting, it came as a shock to learn that this was not so. Not only this but I learned that the building site was over ten hours drive away.

Unfortunately, this unexpected delay dragged on for a number of weeks. When we finally arrived at the site some weeks later not only was there no foundation in but the building materials were still needing to be gathered. No preparation had been done. The misleading communication left me concerned and confused. I did not have the money to stay indefinitely in South Sudan waiting for the project to be organized.

**Christmas Present Prayers**

During the interim before moving to the village where the school would be built, we stayed at the Iris Global Base in Yei, South Sudan. While I couldn't help but be disappointed that my primary reason for coming to South Sudan was at a standstill, it was impossible to be sad with so many happy children around. The young children, who did not have family to call their own, lived on the base. These children were so precious and quickly became my little shadows by day. I loved them all so much, we played and sang together as the days passed and I poured stories and prayers into their lives. These kids had such a joy in their hearts that often it spilled over contagiously into laughter and smiles.

As the holiday season approached it was with sadness to learn that there wasn't enough money to buy Christmas gifts for the children. What should be an especially exciting time was looking quite dismal. As it stood currently, there were no Christmas celebrations or presents for the young ones to anticipate or enjoy.

This touched my heart a lot, and I was sure it was touching God's heart so much more than mine. After all, God was already so involved in loving these children. Hadn't He made sure each one of them found a home where previously they had none? Wasn't He providing for their daily physical and spiritual nourishment, and ongoing education? These practical blessings were a wonderful display of God's goodness. The more I thought of how God was blessing their lives, a song I knew from Ghana came to my memory. The words of this song cheerfully declare, "God, You are good. God, You are kind. God, you are wonderful. My Lord You are excellent!" As the words of the song resounded in my spirit I prayed inwardly, *Lord, I know You love to show Your goodness, why not now?* I felt an expectant faith from God begin to fill me up even as I encouraged the mama's and the kids that God was absolutely going to provide an amazing Christmas, "Tonight, why don't we gather to pray for a special Christmas surprise." And that is just what we did.

How earnestly those children prayed that night and believed Papa God for the impossible to happen. It wasn't just on this night of prayer, in all reality I found myself continually amazed at the way these children earnestly prayed. God was so very real to them and they depended on Him in a way that was incredible to witness. How precious their devotion and what a testimony. As we prayed together that night with no gifts in sight, God was already answering those prayers long before they even left our mouths.

One week later the prayed for blessing came just in time for Christmas. Oh the excitement that came to see a large, mysterious shipment arrive on base. Nobody knew it was coming, in fact it showed up quite unexpectedly. Inside the shipment were so many Christmas presents that there was enough to go around and even more to share with the children in village homes living close by the mission base.

Soon the happy kids were dancing around the compound wearing new

Christmas miracle sandals. Seeing the amount of sheer exuberance over new shoes was delightful. But the children's heartfelt praise and thanksgiving to Papa God to see their prayers answered was by far the best Christmas gift of all that year.

## On to the village

Eventually we moved on to the distant village to start building the school. We worked alongside two local pastors, who assisted us in so many ways and were such a blessing to our lives. As the work moved forward the situation became very turbulent. At times the project would come to a complete stop. Unfortunately, most of the challenges we faced could have been avoided. I found myself deeply concerned. With tact and gentleness the local volunteer workers would have had no cause for offense. However, because this was not the case there were occasions when the men would drop their tools and walk off the job site angry at the way they were being treated. A number of times I found myself having to talk through issues with them, encouraging them to lay down their grievances and pick up their tools again. It pained me a lot, as firsthand I knew what it was like to be on the receiving end of insensitive words and actions.

When we were not busy working on the school, I began to use the freer time to venture out and visit local families in their homes. I loved meeting new people and soon found that a walk up any one of the nearby hills always brought me into contact with friends. The locals of this part of South Sudan live in round mud huts with amazing thatched roofs that point skyward. These roofs were unique in their design. Steep needle-like spikes reached upward as the thatch covering came close to the ground. Boys and men can be seen hunting with bows and arrows or herding large cattle. The women are such hard workers too. Each day these women travel more than five miles with heavy loads of firewood piled high on their heads. They sell this wood in order to feed their families.

One morning I joined a group of girls as they walked along the road with their firewood bundles. Remembering how I used to carry things on my head all the time as a boy, I asked if I could take one of the loads of wood. To this they nodded with smiles of amusement and soon were laughing heartily as I struggled under the weight. My assistance was short lived, and in turn I was filled with additional awe at how strong these girls must be to journey so far with such heavy loads, many of them barefoot too!

Water was extremely scarce in the area. One day some friends took us to see where they go to gather water, I was shocked. It was a small hole hollowed out in the clay, but the water inside the hole did not look like it was good for much of anything. It was thick and brown. Cattle were drinking in the waterhole as we neared. They ambled all over that small waterhole, stomping in the mud and relieving themselves whenever necessary. As soon as the cattle were finished the women would take their turn. Each lady sat patiently by the edge of the water waiting for the cattle to leave. As soon as the mud had somewhat settled to the bottom they carefully eased their buckets into the water and filled them. The water was then carried back home for bathing, cooking, drinking and laundering. It is a wonder that anyone's body could handle the soiled and contaminated water, and yet it was all they had.

In spite of the challenges associated with just staying alive, there was a lot of happiness in the lives of those I met. Time and again I was welcomed into homes with open arms. In the natural I didn't have much to give but found my greatest privilege was always praying for these friends and telling them the story of Jesus. This they appreciated, listening with radiant faces and gladly accepting prayer. As Holy Spirit touched their hearts there were often tears in their eyes. These are some of my most treasured memories of this time.

**A sudden ending**

Prior to leaving the ship in Sierra Leone I had voiced questions regarding the financial logistics of my stay in South Sudan. Each query was eased as I was assured that there was nothing for me to worry about. In fact, all the details and expenses were to be covered under my friend's nonprofit. In contrast to these promises I unexpectedly found myself having to carry many of my own expenses once there. After four months the day arrived when the money I had brought with me was no longer sufficient to support me. So when my friend arrived back at our hut one day after renewing his visa and informed me that I would have to go and pay for my own visa to be extended also, I knew there was no way I could carry this.

While there were those supporting me from abroad, somehow in the handling of others this money never made it to my hands. The money I had with me was meager, I was not capable of financing a furtherance of my stay. What a sad reality to face. Leaving did not feel right at all. The project, which I thought would surely be done by this time, was moving slowly and still had much that needed completing because of the delay.

One of the specific questions I had asked before flying to South Sudan was how I would fly home. My airline ticket to come to this part of the African continent was purchased one-way, and yet, when I had voiced concern, I was assured not to worry myself about the return flight. However, now when I asked about securing an airfare home all I was told was that I would have to figure it out for myself.

Not only was I stunned, I was devastated. The local pastor stood nearby as my friend pulled some cash from his wallet and handed it to me for the long journey home. It may have been a pitiful attempt to right the wrong, but the money alone would not even cover the small bus fare to Yei, South Sudan. It was like a knife to my heart as I left that day. I felt betrayed and forsaken. I had been left completely hanging by my friend whom I had loved as a brother.

I had barely enough money on me to get out of South Sudan and down into Uganda. Boarding the bus I swallowed hard to hold back my tears. The knot tightened in my stomach.

God is a God of miracles and while He could have supernaturally provided for me to stay, in His sovereignty that door closed. The pathway ahead of me had innumerable obstacles to face, but the road behind me had clearly ended. I called a distant friend living in Uganda and with his welcome invitation I started to make the long journey south to his home.

**"We will kill you!"**

Th journey out of South Sudan was sprinkled with many stops. One such stop will forever remain etched into my memory. We arrived at a certain village grateful for a rest from the confines of the bus and jolting of the bumpy road which had resulted in a flat tire. Piling out of our cramped seats the other passengers and I gladly took the opportunity to stretch our legs and walk around a bit. I noticed a few children playing in a nearby tree and waved to them with a smile. While I had not yet taken any picture I was holding my camera in hand. Before I knew what had happened I found myself surrounded by an angry mob of men. They yelled at me and from what small bits of English arose here and there I realized that they thought I was trying to use my camera in some way to harm the children. "We will kill you!" they roared. This was no joke and I could feel the atmosphere around me charging with anger. "My God help me!" I prayed in desperation as my thoughts began to fly. If each man came to fight me separately I might just stand a chance but there were so many of them and they all were coming at once. As the yells progressed to outright punches I knew my situation was dire. No one from the bus dared to come to my aid. If I were to be saved only God Himself could save me.

At this critical moment along the road came a most mysterious man, I had never met him before in my life, for all I knew he was coming to fuel the fire. As the man walked closer he suddenly called out in a loud and authoritative voice. The words rose easily above the angry gathering as this man said, "Leave him alone, he is a man of God!" I find it interesting looking back at this moment that I understood what the man was saying, as did the gang around me even though we all spoke different languages. Instantly, the men surrounding me stopped throwing punches and stepped back a bit. When I looked again to see who this man was, he was gone. I never had a chance to see where the man went. Although there is no natural explanation for this incredible rescue, what I do know is that God used him to help me in my moment of near death.

The mob of men now demanded to see my passport, they were still quite upset though greatly calmed in comparison to moments before. I did not hand my paperwork to them knowing that in seconds they could tear it to shreds and I would have absolutely nothing. Without my passport I couldn't even leave the country, let alone pass through many other countries on my way home. "I'm from Ghana!" I repeated emphatically over and over. But while we were all Africans not one of those men seemed to have any idea where Ghana was. The closest they came to was asking if I meant, "Uganda?" The idea that I was from the neighboring Uganda only served to increase their agitation with me.

At a loss of what to do next, I suddenly remembered that instead of my usual black socks I was wearing a white pair of tourist socks from Ghana. The socks were covered in brightly colored Ghanaian flags. Thank Jesus for tourist socks! To this day I believe it was the grace of God to have me wear those socks that day. Kicking off my shoe, I pulled up a pant leg and pointed at my socks. Curiosity prevailed as the men looked down to see why on earth my shoes were flying off my feet. Suddenly their anger evaporated almost as fast as it had come, instead, they started laughing and chanting happily, "GHaNaaa! Oh you are GHaNaa!" Ghana is well known for their soccer team and so when the men saw that I was from Ghana they also saw that I was not a threat to them or their community, in fact they liked Ghana. I couldn't thank God enough for my stinky socks. About this time a local policeman showed up on the scene and I felt safe to hand him my passport. I was so grateful and ready to climb back on the bus and continue on my way.

# Chapter 12 - Providential Moving

"I will go before you,
And make the crooked places straight."
~ Isaiah 45:2 ~

After many hours we finally arrived at a bus station on the border of Uganda. I made my way off the bus and walked along the curbside to wait for the next bus to arrive and take us further down into Uganda. As I walked along a young man walking in front of me suddenly dropped what appeared to be a large bundle of money. It landed right in my pathway and was impossible to miss. Instead of bending over to pick it up I stood looking at it, there was a bell of caution ringing inside my spirit which made me hesitate. Holy Spirit was prompting me to leave the money alone. "Pick up the money." an audible voice from behind urged me. I turned around quickly to see who could be standing so close at my back, it was a youth of about eighteen years. "I won't pick it up, it's not mine." I replied and promptly called loudly after the one who had dropped the money. "Why don't you keep it?" The youth urged again. "God provides, I don't have to steal to be blessed." I replied.

From the look on his face he was obviously not expecting this reply and went on to ask what I meant. I began to talk with him about Jesus. We were still chatting together even as the first young man who dropped the money strolled cautiously back towards us, more than a little confused. He reached down and picked up the wad still lying on the ground. As he did so I noticed that it was not money at all, rather it was only a stack of papers made to look a little like money. I overheard the first guy mutter, "Not this one, we'll leave him alone." Thankfully by obeying the quiet prompting of Holy Spirit not only had God spared me from disaster once more, but also provided an opening to share Jesus. Sometime later I learned that it is quite common in this area of Uganda for armed robbers to work in pairs. One will drop a bait for the unsuspecting victim, while the other comes up from behind and attacks.

To say that I was relieved to arrive at my Ugandan friend's home would be an understatement. It was more like one surely must feel finding an oasis in some wilderness land. My friend welcomed me with open arms. As we sat down to eat that evening's meal he told me about his school which would start for him immediately. "The school is not open to visitors, so I'm afraid you cannot stay with me." Noticing the perplexed look on my face, he quickly added that he was sure I might be able to go and stay with his local pastor. "Perhaps you can remain in my pastor's home until you figure out what to do next." He encouraged me. With the circumstances I was up against, this sounded like a good idea.

When the pastor was contacted however, we found out that he was on a distant journey and wouldn't return for quite some time. My friend was distressed to hear this news as there really wasn't much else he could do to help me. We said goodbye the next morning. I had no choice left but to take more of my fleeting money and use it to travel back from where I'd just come the day prior in Kampala, Uganda's capital. This is where the airport was and though I had no more contacts in the city, or the country for that matter, it seemed the place to go. I must trust God and pray for a good outcome.

## "God, are You there?"

On the ride back to Kampala I felt so alone in life. I was literally going in circles and had no clue what my next decision should or could be when the time came to hop off the bus. The truth was I had run clean out of options and quickly was running out of cash too. Africa is an extremely big continent filled with many countries whose cultures and languages are vastly foreign, home seemed further away than it had ever been. Sighing heavily and trying to calm a growing sense of panic I closed my eyes and tried to focus on the steady hum of the engine. *God, are You there?* I prayed silently, *Papa God, I need to know You are with me now.* I squeezed my eyes tightly shut as I felt His still small voice speak comfortingly, "Son, I am holding you now."

When the bus arrived in the large metropolis of Kampala I climbed off and followed the dispersing crowd for a short way. I had decided against staying in hotels, as this would surely finish my money in one moment. Sleeping on the street would have to do. As I scouted out a place that would be safe to stay that night, the delicious smells of food from a passing street vendor caught my nose. It smelled so good and no longer could I push away the reality that I was hungry. I quickly walked the other way. Now was not the time to eat, rather it was the time more than ever before to ration what was left inside my pocket.

Instead of eating, I walked into a small internet cafe and sat down at a computer. Opening my email account a few names of individuals passed randomly through my thoughts. Was there someone I could write to that might be able to help? Glancing at the screen I noticed a new message in my inbox. Looking again in amazement, I saw that of all unexpected things it was a notice from an international money transferring agency informing me that 50 dollars had been wired directly to me and was ready to pick up at any Ugandan bank.

More surprising to me than anything else however was the fact that this money had been sent from none other than Bobbi. This completely stunned me. Bobbi had never sent money like this, and, truth be told, I hadn't spoken or written to her in a very long time. While we were friends on the ship I clearly believed that there was no future for us. I was completely sure she would soon fade from my memory, certain too that I would fade from hers. And yet, here she was blessing me and doing anything but fading away. Bobbi had written an email as well, and as I read the words she wrote it was as if she were right beside me, understanding firsthand what I was facing and exactly what encouragement my heart needed. And yet, apart from a miracle, Bobbi had no earthly way of knowing what I was going through at this very minute, or how much of a timely blessing it was for me to receive this message and the money.

The day was swiftly coming to a close and so, without waiting a second longer, I jumped up from the chair and went straight to the closest bank to withdraw the funds. From the bank I made a beeline for that food vendor and was soon enjoying a hot meal praising God and thanking Him for this timely provision. It seemed as though each bite of food was accompanied with thoughts of Bobbi who seemed so close and yet was living half a world away. How could she know? Why did she do that? Why did she even care?

I couldn't sleep that night but it wasn't the city noises, the foreign culture or anything else around me that kept me awake. My thoughts were far too busy trying to solve the dilemma ahead of me. As the hours passed, I cried out to God for wisdom and He faithfully responded. When the random idea came to call a certain pastor in South Sudan, I quickly pulled out my phone and dialed the number. The pastor was a prayerful man and was more than happy to pray with me. Just about the time when we were going to hang up he said, "Wait a minute, did you know that David from the Iris base is going to Kampala?" I had not heard this. The pastor continued, "Well, why don't you contact him, perhaps there is something he can help you with."

**Above and beyond**

Hanging up the phone I dialed David's number. Even though the hour was very late David picked up the call. I listened to his cheerful voice greeting me on the other end of the line. I explained briefly to him about my current situation and that's when he interjected me with, "Michael just wait a minute." A short time later he returned on the line to say, "Right now I am in Kampala with one of the boys. He has a document to pick up and after that we'll head back across the border. I've just spoken with our hotel manager and you are welcome to come and stay with us until we have to leave."

Meeting David in Kampala was a direct answer to prayer. He blessed me tremendously and bought me breakfast that next morning. As we ate, we spoke about many things. David has a real father's heart and in those moments of distress he poured such love and encouragement into my life. As he prayed and prophesied over me I sat there at the breakfast table and began to cry. My tears were ones of gratefulness to have someone understand deeply and care for me practically. In fact, I was overwhelmed with the love of God displayed through my friend. The sweet presence of Holy Spirit drew so close in that hotel dining room. I still didn't know how to surpass the mountain in front of me, I had no idea at all how to make my way home. But as David prayed I could feel my spirit rising up in hope of what the Lord was going to do in the midst of my need. I was so grateful when David unexpectedly handed me a key to my own hotel room. It was a nice room, far surpassing the noisy streets outside, and in the privacy of my quiet room I set myself to pray through the night. The following morning I confidently spoke to the young boy traveling with David, "I'm praying that God is going to bless you with your document on the very same day that I have a flight to Ghana."

Just to clarify a little, while there are plenty of banks all over Africa, transferring money from bank to bank across a multitude of countries was slow and challenging at best and impossible at worst. I still had a few funds in my Ghanaian bank account which I desperately needed to access, even though I didn't know if it would be sufficient to purchase a flight.

God is so good, over the next week a multitude of miracles happened. He gave me outstanding favor when I contacted a local Ugandan bank, the bank was able and willing to directly speak to my bank in Ghana. God was on the move and all things were becoming efficient and possible. Within the week, the two banks were able to connect successfully to the point that my entire savings account was released and transferred from the country of Ghana all the way to Uganda. This was a huge miracle. Also, before the week was out I was able to take the transferred money to a travel agency and by the grace of God I had just enough to book a flight that was leaving the very next day for Ghana. All week I had food to eat and a comfortable place to stay with friends. The last miracle unfolded Friday morning, the day I was to leave. My friends finally received their much anticipated but delayed document and were able to return home to South Sudan.

**To love or to hate**

On the flight home I had plenty of time to think. After all God had so miraculously done for me I sadly didn't choose to think about the blessings. Instead I began to go over the many negative experiences that had happened to me. The more I thought about these negative and painful things the more dark sad memories flooded in. A few of them I have written about here in my story but most I have decided are best left unsaid. The unfortunate memories I was focused on filled me with poison until all the light was squeezed out. The devil was quick to take advantage of my dismal contemplation. It was as though a waterfall flooded into my mind of all the injustices I had received from white people. This rapid downward spiral progressed as the enemy continued seeding hatred; he wanted it planted firmly in my heart.

Face after face, fact upon fact and memory after painful memory crowded in. It all battled for a chance to take the stage under the limelight of hurt and offense. I wish I could say I drew near to God in this battle, resisted the devil and rose above that rugged terrain as easily as our plane now soared over the African landscape below, but this wasn't the case. I didn't resist him one bit. But the more I chose to dwell on the painful experiences of my life, the angrier I became. By the time we landed in Kenya for our layover, I was outright furious. Mad to the point that I had determined I would punch any white person who crossed my path.

How quickly this dismal struggle with my thoughts had become a losing battle.

I was like Peter sinking in the sea. He too found himself in deep waters as his focus left Jesus and settled instead on the storm surrounding his life. My own sinking state happened so quickly. While the injustices I fumed about were from others, wallowing in anger and offense was my choice. I was miserable and yet it all felt so justifiable. It's a somber realization to understand that the very thing which causes us pain, like hatred, can soon be held in our own hearts and embraced with such disastrous self-righteousness. Thank God for Jesus. In my sinking place God remained so faithful. With what happened next I could say He quickly came to the rescue, and yet I know that in fact He never left. God was always right there the entire time extending His merciful hand to pull me out of the mire I was so stuck in.

And so there I sat fuming in the layover waiting area of some Kenyan airport, lost in all the inner turmoil and not paying the least attention to my surroundings. It was an upsetting surprise to hear a woman's voice addressing me. Even more upsetting to look up and see a very white lady and her very white daughter looking down at me. I know God had sent them and yet in that moment they were the last people I wanted to meet. Both mother and daughter were smiling happily and asking me a question. To this day I don't remember the simple question they asked. All I can recall is how difficult it was for me to respond to them.

Angry as I was, I could hear the calm whisper of the Holy Spirit calling me up higher. Through these two women God was offering me a way of escape through the door of loving forgiveness. I knew that to respond to these white humans kindly would mean going through the door of forgiveness. I had told others about this door many times, I knew that freedom would only be found in letting go and surrendering to God all the bitterness that was consuming my heart. I had a choice to make; either choose love and answer nicely, or stubbornly hold onto my miserable feelings and hurt someone. Thankfully, I made the best decision that day. As I responded in love and answered the woman's question it was as if instantly a noose around my neck was released. All the bitter racial hate, so desperately trying to gain footing in my heart, left as the light of Jesus illuminated my soul once more. I was undone and so relieved as this burden was lifted from my life and I felt free.

The choice is always ours to make, I can heartily say that choosing love over hatred is by far the best choice. In fact, hatred should never be an option we choose. No matter how justified in holding bitterness, it is a poison that destroys us from the inside out. When Jesus was on the earth He advised His followers time and again to forgive the very ones who had hurt them. He knew that forgiveness is not just the key out of the offense's dark house, it is also the key to open the stronghold of God's radiant love.

## Back to Kumasi

Over a year had passed since leaving Ghana. I arrived back to Kumasi, the bustling garden city of my homeland, with a thankfulness towards God for His incredible mercy, love, and protection. Throughout the year that was now behind, God had shown me like never before just how powerful He is.

It was the miraculous power of God that mercifully brought me home, and He did so in part by allowing me to withdraw those savings from my account and use it for a plane ticket. This blessing of the past carried with it the opportunity at present to learn even more about trusting God completely as my provider. In the natural I returned to Ghana entirely destitute financially. What little money I had diligently tried to save over the years for my own home and future was now gone. There was nothing left to start over with and I quickly found that in my culture where business is mostly via personal referrals (and I had been away for a long time), finding work as an electrician was challenging and slow.

I clearly saw and felt these challenges. It was not uncommon to spend a mealtime with an empty plate, but this did not dampen my hope. God was faithful to me and often those hungry moments became opportunities to fast and feed on the promises of my Heavenly Father. I may have missed a meal but I never missed the joy of seeing how God always filled me up with strength. Sometimes I was hungry, yes, but by God's grace I was never weak. With or without calories inside, I always had plenty of energy during the day and night. Thankfully the Holy Spirit touched a few loving church mama's who blessed me with a cooked meal here and there. I moved back to a vacant room on the church compound and was soon as busy as ever.

While it didn't take long for me to settle once more into the routine of life in my own country, I now entered each day with a renewed sense of purpose. My history with Papa God only increased my desire to spend as much time with Him in prayer as I could find. As I devoted myself with renewed passion to spending time in prayer and fasting, I would often lead out in prayer evenings, prayer all-nights, and prayer before services at the church.

**Like a heavy fist**

Soon after resuming life and tasks at the church an additional responsibility was given to me. Each Sunday I would take the church van and drive around the city to pick up members for the day's service. I loved driving the large passenger van. It didn't take long for the bus to fill to the brim with happy churchgoers and together we would often sing and talk our way back to the church. Nevertheless as nice as it was, this responsibility would only be short lived.

One morning I awoke with a start. *What on earth is going on?* My heart was still pounding as with a great sigh of relief I realized it had only been a very bad dream. In the dream I was driving the van when all at once a large giant entered my way and slammed his giant fist onto the hood of the van. It was a nasty and vicious accident. A few days after this dreadful dream my good friend of many years, and now associate pastor of the church, Charles B. called me aside. "Michael, last night I had a dream and it concerned me a lot." He said. "What was the dream?" I asked him curiously. As he explained the dream I couldn't help but realize that it was much like the dream I had experienced

121

earlier. "Michael, we need to pray. I feel we need to seriously pray about this." Pastor B. shook his head, "It was a serious dream my brother." We prayed about these dreams believing the Lord to cancel every intention the enemy may have.

The next Sunday came with a lot of sunshine. It was a fine day for driving and I was full of joy. *What a great day to worship with others!* I thought as I jumped into the driver's seat and wove my way into the traffic. The first young lady I picked up hopped in the front seat and immediately began to talk about vehicle accidents. Remembering my dream I quickly put the thought aside and determined to be extra careful. Greeting each person as they hopped into the van we were soon packed in and ready to head back to the church. The van was full of mamas and children, all squeezing in as best they could. Nobody wore a seatbelt as the van was not equipped with seat belts. Ghana did not require them in all vehicles.

Suddenly, out of nowhere a small car crossed into my path, it veered right in front of us as if it hadn't even noticed our van. I slammed on the brakes and swung the van's steering wheel in a desperate attempt to avoid hitting the driver's side door. Our van collided directly with the rear side of the oncoming car. Immediately both vehicles spun completely out of control. The van was rolling over and over, while the small car flipped into the oncoming traffic. It was surreal and terrible.

Back at the church the worship team was preparing to begin when the pastor was informed that the local radio station had announced an accident involving our church's van. The radio mentioned that all the passengers and the driver were dead on impact. This was devastating news to try and start the service with.

Thank God that His report was better than the radio's report. Back at the scene of the accident, we finally came to a stop with the van on its side, wheels still spinning in the air. The fact that there were no cars in the oncoming lanes was a miracle for the other driver and his squashed car. In the distance I saw the driver of the small car begin to safely emerge from his wreckage. My thoughts were dreading what may have become of my own passengers. I felt sick to my stomach and weak in my knees. However, another miracle happened as each mama and each child was helped out from our demolished van, in fact not one person was killed.

Supernaturally, by the grace of God, everyone was able to walk away from the accident that day. The worst injuries among us were only some missing teeth, scrapes and bruises. Blood was coming from my hands and my shoulder was in pain but I also experienced no major injuries. The accident was shocking and yet God totally saved us in His mercy.

Back at the church, everyone's devastation turned to joyful thanksgiving when we all showed up sometime later. The van was gone for good, but we were safe and sound. This incident once again reinforced in my mind the vital importance of setting everything, known or unknown, past, present or future, before God in prayer.

**Important pursuit**

It was after the van accident that I really began to think about what was important in life. I was thirty three years old and as single as the day I turned one. I knew in my heart that God would bring me the right partner at the right time. While I was not worried about my future in regards to finding a wife, it was not uncommon for good intentioned mamas from church, and many others along the way, to point out eligible young ladies and try their very best to advise me into what they thought would be a match made in heaven. Nevertheless, I had fully determined I would not rush into marriage.

I had a great contentment in my spirit with my relationship with God. I wouldn't trade this friendship with Him for anything else in this world. God knew the plans He had for me and slowly began the process of opening a place in my heart for a wife. As I prayed for my future wife and wondered who this could be, Bobbi would often come to mind. She was the one person who had remained a faithful friend and constant encourager to me over the past eighteen months since we parted as friends on the Mercy Ship. Time and again her messages had found me at moments when I needed an encouraging word the most. By contrast I had not been replying. Someone needed to change and that someone was me.

I started to email Bobbi on a regular basis and still remember the day I asked if we could speak over the phone. On our second phone conversation I boldly gathered courage to ask her if she had a boyfriend. When I heard her say that she did not have someone in her life, a smile of hope rose from my heart and settled on my face. I could almost see that heaven must be smiling too.

In many ways it seemed impossible to even imagine a serious relationship with someone who lived so far away and had grown up in about as different a culture as is possible to imagine. Our friendship was indeed growing which was wonderful, but more than anything I needed confirmation from God. We prayed so much for Him to guide both of our steps and asked counsel from loved ones and respected friends. We both believed that marriage is a serious covenant before God and not to be entered into lightly.

There were still months to wait before we could meet each other face to face, but the anticipated reunion, hopes for the future and love that God was stirring in our hearts kept us close even though we remained half a world apart. As I waited those intervening months, how little did I realize that right around the next corner a long hoped for dream was just about to take place.

# Chapter 13 - Return to Sweet Salone

"Remember the word to your servant,
Upon which You have caused me to hope."
~ Psalm 119:49 ~

I hadn't seen it coming, but here it was miraculously placed right in my hand! One round-trip airfare to Sierra Leone scheduled for the very next month. "Thank You God!" I exclaimed. The words bounced themselves off the cement walls and brightly painted red mailboxes of Kumasi's large two storied post office, even as a few bystanders glanced curiously towards my direction. Gratefully I clutched the papers in my hand, soon to be my reality was a cherished dream.

Ever since leaving the ship, I had received multiple invitations by friends and pastors in Sierra Leone to come back to their country to help with ministry. I longed to return to the place and people who had become so dear to me. But up until this very moment such a journey was not even plausible. The small money that did come into my possession always seemed to leave even quicker to pay for the bare essentials of daily life. There was nothing extra to work with, let alone travel with. God however has limitless resources and as I looked at that incredible gift of an airfare, I was reminded once again that nothing is too impossible for Him. Soon I would be on my way for a month of ministry in the country of 'Sweet Salone.'

**A wing and a prayer**

Securing myself into the small seat of the airplane, I relaxed and looked out the window at the bustle of activity below as our luggage was being stowed in the hold. I couldn't help but laugh aloud as the memories of my first flight to Mozambique flashed across my mind, I sure wasn't relaxed then. Thank God for new seasons. Pulling out my phone I sent a last text to Bobbi before takeoff and then switched the phone off. It was such a precious joy to have her in my life. Placing the phone back in my pocket I suddenly felt the crinkly texture of money. *50 dollars is all that's in there,* I thought with a cringe. All the money that I had to cover every expense over the next month's mission. *I will be as frugal as I can, but still, is this amount going to stretch the distance of days?* I certainly did not wish for a second monetary predicament in a foreign country. God calmly spoke to my spirit, "Son, whatever it costs you it will also cost Me."

The flight up the west coast of Africa ended perfectly as we landed safely in Freetown's airport. Soon the salty spray of ocean water could be felt in the air, it was refreshing to be back in Sierra Leone and I was hopeful for all that would take place in the coming days. One of the local pastors had offered to host me in his home for the duration of this month and I was grateful. It was a simple home and yet comfortable for me.

Even though they are relatively close to one another, the countries of Ghana and Sierra Leone have many cultural differences. Knowing how important it is to adapt to cultural differences, there was one thing I struggled with and simply couldn't budge on. Most toilets in Sierra Leone didn't have toilet paper. Water may have been the alternative, but the bottom line for me was that in this regard I would not adapt, I insisted on toilet paper. One of my first trips to the market was to find this vital commodity.

As I searched the market tables for the necessary roll of tissue, I thought back to my childhood in Dakojum village. We didn't even have a toilet in our one room home. When nature called, you just had to walk the distance out of the house and go into the bush to relieve yourself, or pay to use the village wash house. One may wonder, with no inside toilet, did we have toilet paper? That's a very good question. And yet even in that primitive circumstance we did have toilet paper, although it was not the typical kind. My mother would sometimes come home with rags of material from a local tailor and we would use these discarded cloths as our tissue. While it may seem strange, those odd shaped rags were actually a luxury in our home for they far surpassed our more common option of old corn cobs and their husks. Corn cobs were hardly comfortable for the job, but it worked effectively, and we had our paper. That being said, I'm grateful for the modern convenience of genuine toilet paper. That day in the hot Sierra Leone market I bought the first roll I could find and last one in sight.

It was good to settle in Sierra Leone even if for four swiftly passing weeks. Soon I was joining friends as we traveled to preach, pray and encourage their local communities and churches. When a call came from another pastor friend of mine, I was eager to accept his invitation to come and speak at a village church. I went to his church that first evening and we had a wonderful service. The Lord really blessed the message and afterwards there were plenty of people who came forward for individual prayers. Among these were some men and women from a religion that was not christian. These hungry ones were totally set free that night and experienced the power and love of Jesus Christ even as they accepted Him into their hearts. I left with high hopes of returning the next evening.

However, the result of that first night stirred up a lot of resistance to the point of having to cancel the second night. Instead we gathered to pray for the breakthrough we would need before we could proceed with another meeting. By God's grace the next evening's service went remarkably well. There were no disruptions, and, in fact, a lot of Holy Spirit's blessing was present even as more people encountered Jesus for the first time. I could hardly believe the peaceful atmosphere. Prayer is powerful - darkness cannot handle it.

**Pink, blue and lollipops too**

"It's a long way but we'll make it!" My host pastor smiled broadly. "On that?" I asked in amazement. We all burst out laughing as the pastor nodded, confidently pointing to a small motorcycle off to one side of the road. The bike sat empty, waiting calmly for all four of us; pastor, friend, driver, and I to hop on. "Well then, I guess there's only one way to find out if it's going to work." I took a gullible step toward the bike and with that we all climbed cautiously on the two wheels that were going to take us across the miles and to the village. I made sure to sit on the very back just in case I decided to bail off.

*Pastor you sure weren't joking!* I thought to myself as hours of potholed roads later we climbed stiffly off the bike and gratefully stretched our cramped legs. The raucous arrival of our overcrowded motorbike sparked an avalanche of welcomes from a growing crowd of villagers. They were happy and curious to see us and soon waited quietly as the pastor stood up to make the introductions. I stood beside him, smiling at the happy faces in front of me.

All at once I heard the pastor say something to the village chief in the hearing of everyone. What he said just about made me fall over right there on the spot. I choked back a gasp as I heard him continue, "And so yes please, bring all the children, because our guest Michael from Ghana is going to bless every single child in this village with a new school uniform!" *A what?? I've never even talked about giving anything, let alone giving every child a uniform. Does he even have any idea how much that would cost?* My thoughts were panicked ones. I didn't even have the money to buy one uniform, let alone what had just been promised.

I anxiously scanned the crowd. It seemed to me that children were multiplying on the scene like the loaves and fishes in the bible. *What am I going to do?* I lamented inwardly knowing all too well how serious a promise is taken in Africa. Before I even had a chance to address the misunderstanding with the pastor over a hundred children were milling about me. They were happy and excited at the thought of new uniforms for school. All of them were laughing, smiling and coming to shake my hand. *I can't possibly tell them now!* I thought even as a parent approached me with tears of gratitude in her eyes. Almost the entire village was Muslim, they were shocked to see a Christian willing to bless them in this way. Little did they know the practical predicament of the Christian who stood in front of them.

We left that day amid waves and shouts of joy. Affirmations filled the air of our soon return to the village with a tailor ready to take the children's measurements. I jumped on that motorcycle quicker than ever, and began to pray for a miracle. I couldn't bail out now! I prayed all the way home and continued praying throughout the night. Before leaving for Sierra Leone I had emailed a number of friends to inform them of my mission. However, I had not heard back from most nor had I received anything by way of financial support. I was not going to beg them for money, and yet money is exactly what was so desperately needed.

As I struggled to know what to practically do, I was reminded of what God had shared with me on my way to Sierra Leone, "Son, whatever it costs you it will also cost Me." This was the key. The memory caused me to hope in God and start to move forward in faith. I did have money to hire a tailor for one day and decided to trust God to provide what was needed beyond that. A tailor was soon found quite willing to go with us, so many uniforms meant a lot of income for him and he was delighted. I doubt he would have been so eager had he known the lack of cash in my pocket. Back we went over the potholes, tailor in tow, to the village. The measurements were made in the school building as every joyful youngster squeezed into the sweltering tin roofed building, it was hard to concentrate on anything except laughing at their happy antics.

That evening I gratefully closed the door to my room ready to relax. It had been a long, successful day of measurements but exhausting all the same. Before sleeping I decided to check my email and in doing so shouted in amazement. I saw that not one, but three friends from three different locations had quite unexpectedly sent financial blessings for the mission in Sierra Leone. Not last week, not yesterday, but this day just in time! *Thank You God, Your timing is impeccable! Oh thank You, thank You Jesus!* My sleep was extra restful that night as I drifted off with renewed gratefulness for God's blessing that had come at the perfect time through my friends. As I collected the funds that very next morning I kept thinking about how God knows just how to move our mountains in the right time in order to build our trust and faith in Him. How He delights in blowing us away with His goodness. I was blown away.

The uniforms were the blessing God used to break open the door for the gospel in that village. Many were touched as they saw the love of Jesus displayed so practically for their families. As for the money that came? The combined amount was just what was needed. There was enough money to cover the yardage of blue and pink material, enough money to pay the tailor to sew all those uniforms, and, can you believe it? There was even enough money left over to buy two hundred lollipops to share with the children. Why? Because yes, God is that good. He's a God of provision, but beyond that, He is our above and 'immeasurably more' God. And for this time, far away in that village, God's 'immeasurably more' goodness took the shape of sweet lollipops.

**Brother for life**

His suit was starched, his tie brightly brilliant and his large watch sparkled precisely with the time. What a contrast to my far from fancy attire. I had intentionally avoided suits my entire life and was quite proud of the fact. However, while hard to miss, it wasn't this brother's impeccable style that impressed me that day when I first saw him in the church. But rather, it was his passion and fire for God, which soon became very evident to all of us in the room. When he spoke, the words resounded with clarity and boldness and he carried such a gift of prophetic insight. His style was quite outspoken but his spirit was very humble.

After the service we were introduced by a mutual friend, I learned that this brother's name was Sheka. He too was visiting the country but also was a citizen of Sierra Leone. He had moved as a young boy to the United States during the devastating years of war that ravaged his country, and had since grown up in America. This was his first visit back home in many years and yet like myself he also was only staying in Sierra Leone for one month. In spite of our extremely differing preferences in the fashion department, and while both of us lived on different continents, our friendship was instant. The brotherly bond between us was the grace of God and for us to meet there in Sierra Leone a true divine appointment.

When I first told Sheka my name and he learned I was from Ghana, my new friend's eyes opened wide and he began to smile. "Glory to God, thank You Jesus!" He exclaimed, proceeding to open his bible and pull out a small piece of notepaper. I listened curiously as Sheka began to share with me how prior to this journey to Sierra Leone the Lord had spoken to him very specifically. Not wanting to forget, he had written a simple note to himself and put it inside his bible. In surprise I looked down to see three words scrawled across the paper reading, "Ghana, brother, Michael" During the remaining couple weeks of our time in Sierra Leone we paired up in ministry and watched as God radically blessed. Our paths would soon separate but both of us knew that our friendship was far from over. This was merely the beginning of something glorious that God had planned all along.

**A time to say goodbye**

How quickly one month flew by. I could hardly believe that it was time to say goodbye to Sierra Leone. Climbing up the gangway of the cumbersome Freetown ferry I looked back towards the dock to wave at my friends below. As the ferry pulled away from the shore my eyes made their way across the water to the distant side of the bay. Somewhere over there was the airport and I knew my plane was waiting. The past four weeks had been wonderfully refreshing. Such a gift from God and I was so grateful for His leading, provision and faithfulness. In such a short time I had reconnected with and met so many good friends, I was already missing them all.

As the ferry made its way steadily through that salty seawater I scanned the rapidly disappearing shore from which we had just come. I tried to picture in my mind's eye the outline of a very special hospital ship, long since departed for a new mission far away. In many ways it felt like a lifetime ago when I called the ship home, but really it hadn't been so long ago at all. *How swiftly the seasons of life sail on by,* I thought to myself.

Soon I was flying high in the sky on my way back to Ghana. Yes, I was sad to say goodbye to friends in Sierra Leone, but I couldn't help anticipating the coming days. I was eager to return home to prepare for my sweetest friend who was set to arrive in only two short months.

# Chapter 14 - Home Sweet Home

**"The greatest of these is love."**
**~ 1 Corinthians 13 ~**

"That one right there please!" I said pointing towards the biggest bouquet of red rosebuds I could see. I wanted nothing but the biggest and best bouquet for my sweetheart Bobbi when she arrived. She was coming! I could barely believe that the time of her arrival was mere hours away. Right this very minute she was up there in the sky heading straight my way. I looked hopefully across the silent blue skyline as the florist pulled the vibrant bunch of flowers down and wrapped the plastic buds securely into crunchy tissue paper. Handing over the money I put the bouquet safely inside my backpack and zipped it shut.

Plastic flowers may seem odd to buy for a gift, but in Ghana this is what florists sell. Ghana lacks no flowers mind you, in fact, there are plenty of flowers growing here and there, but truth be told, most Ghanaian ladies do not like fresh flowers the way that many western women do. Flowers aren't seen as practical and most Ghanaians prefer something viewed as useful like plantains, a chicken or some rice. When at times flowers are bought, it is usually a one time occasion and plastic is often the material of choice. These unfading plastic displays, purchased primarily for weddings, last long after real flowers wither away. The colorful bouquets often end up becoming mementos used as decor in a family living room for many years.

With the flowers safely stuffed in my backpack, it didn't take long to stop a taxi and return to my friend's home in Accra to wait for Bobbi's arrival. These friends were missionaries from the United States, and were very accustomed to incoming flight delays from afar. I, on the other hand, was quite the novice; the afternoon couldn't pass fast enough. I was ready to be out the door and at the airport well in advance of the plane's arrival. My friends tried their best to calm me down with the fact that planes into Accra are almost always hours late and there really was no rush at all. I tried my best to be patient but it was hard work.

Finally after much anticipation we entered the airport and joined the large crowd in the arrivals lounge. I held tightly to the roses and looked intently through the glass as each passenger walked out of the customs area and down the long passageway to the open doors. All at once I saw her. Bobbi entered the long hallway looking more beautiful to me than ever. I started to shout her name but while I could see her, she could neither see nor hear me due to a large pane of two way glass separating us. As she walked along that passageway she was obviously wrestling with her luggage. The heaviest and largest bag kept falling from her shoulder and dropping down to the ground. How I wanted to run in and pick up her bags but I wasn't allowed through to help. Instead I just had to helplessly wait and watch in vain as she struggled on to the doors that separated us. I could barely stand still a minute longer. I was excited to see her, desperate to assist and nervous all in one.

And then she walked through the door. Right there in the doorway the bag fell once again but instead of helping pick the bag up as planned I picked her up, which was by far the obvious and best choice in the moment. She was all smiles and as I gave her the flowers, she smiled even more. Soon introductions were made with my friends and we were all set to leave for the house. During the drive home that night Bobbi and I sat in the back of the car. My friends talked to Bobbi the entire way home. She had no time to relax, or even be refreshed by a drink of water. Bobbi didn't seem phased at all as she kept right up with the conversation like it was the most normal thing in the world. As for me I sat there nervous and silent.

We arrived home and I showed Bobbi to a seat at the table where she could now relax. Hurrying into the kitchen I poured a cool glass of water and returned to my waiting friend. *She must see how we properly welcome people to Ghana,* I thought to myself. In the valiant attempt to do everything perfectly I still found myself more nervous than ever, my hand was shaking to the point that instead of calmly putting the glass of water gently on the table instead I knocked it over. Splash! Crash! Water went everywhere as the glass toppled unromantically to the ground. I was horrified. *This is as far from polite as it gets!* Embarrassing though it was for me, it was a great ice-breaker that helped shatter my nervousness and relax us both as we laughed together.

Actually in no time at all Bobbi and I happily adjusted to our friendship, being so much closer than over 7000 miles apart. After a couple days with our friends in Accra we took a bus back to Kumasi and Bobbi moved into a guest house in town.

Looking back I don't know what I was thinking of at the time but decided to test Bobbi's level of patience. I knew marriage had its ups and downs and I guess I wanted to find out what kind of wife she would be under pressure. The following day I intentionally arrived two hours later than arranged to pick her up. She was a little puzzled at the long delay but didn't seem flustered at all. Immediately I regretted the time I'd lost being with her that day.

Only the pastors and my closest friends knew about Bobbi coming to visit. That very first weekend at the church was delightful. I can't even begin to count all the teasing, questions, laughter, whispering and curious stares about who this friend of mine was. Where did she come from and how on earth hadn't they known about her? The church mamas had pressured me for years to find a wife, but they were not at all ready for me to show up with my future one. I thoroughly enjoyed the shock and surprise of the moment.

### "Will you marry me?"

My friend Mike is a smart guy with a big sense of humor. He came over after that first church service to greet us. "So, have you proposed Michael?" he asked me with a grin dancing across his face. Leaning over Mike jabbed me in the ribs while simultaneously letting out a laugh. Obviously something was strange with his question but I had no idea what was so funny. I replied, "Well, ahh yes. Yes I have." Upon hearing my response, Bobbi poked my other side with a very confused look on her face. "Sweets?" She whispered, "No, you haven't. We need to talk." Bobbi's reply made me even more bewildered. Upon seeing this confusion of cultures play out my friend Mike doubled over in laughter. "Michael, trust me I think you still need to propose."

In Ghanaian culture the marriage proposal happens at the start of a relationship. When the man says, "I love you," in Ghana those are the words of proposal and if the endearing sentiment is accepted the young lady becomes your fiancé. What a contrast from America where when someone proposes it is not before, but rather after the relationship has grown. In my mind I had already done all this and viewed Bobbi as my fiancé. Neither Bobbi nor I had a clue about our cultural conflict. But fortunately my friend helped us figure it out.

All this being said, the following week I made a point to propose to Bobbi the western way. It was a terrible disaster. I said many long and loving things to her, except to ask the one question she expected to hear from me. Finally in exasperation she interrupted to ask me, "Are you trying to propose?" "Yes!" I replied *'and it's hard work too'* I thought. Without another word she smiled and just kept sitting there quietly waiting. *What is she waiting for?* My mind was a jumble of confusion, growing by the second. Hadn't I just assured her that this was the proposal? All I could think to myself was, *Those poor men in the west, thank God for simple Ghanaian proposals.* Finally, in amused exasperation Bobbi helped me out, "Michael, but you have to ask me... 'will you marry me?'" "Wait... that's all?" I asked her in shock. Things were already a mess but I went for it anyway, "Bobbi, will you marry me?" With a happy sigh of what appeared to be as much relief as anything else Bobbi smiled and said "Yes, of course!"

I quickly decided that this proposal was far too much of a disaster to count as the only proposal my sweet Bobbi would have. I made up my mind to try one more time. When Bobbi declared her joy at our engagement a few days later, I turned and said, "What are you talking about, we are not engaged.". She stopped and looked at me as if I was crazy, "But you proposed already, just the other day?!" she gasped. I squeezed her hand and quickly assured her, "Oh but that wasn't my proposal. That was my proposal rehearsal, now you just leave it with me and try to be patient." Within that very week I proposed again for the final time making sure to mark the occasion with the proper gifts, accolades and flowers. And last but not least, I remembered to ask that one simple, but all important question, "Will you marry me?" And I thank God that she said yes again.

We were married on a beautiful Sunday morning, the fifth of May, 2013. Heavy rain from the night before had left the grass surrounding the church sparkling in the morning sun. Rain is a blessing and to have the rain the very morning of our wedding was like showers of blessing over our marriage. It was a glorious and memorable day.

**Home sweet home**

We soon set up our home in a simple apartment God totally handpicked for us. In fact, recall the old mission house where the tent church had been, along with the shipping container my friends and I, so many years previous, had called home? Well, all the missionaries had long since moved away from this land and now the mission house was occupied by a local pastor. This older man was not married and due to work he traveled much of the time, only staying at the house when he was in the area. On the side of the mission house was a small apartment and this became our first home. It was just right for us.

Life didn't slow down at all after we were married, in fact, it felt as though everything started to go faster now that there were two of us. Throughout the week I was still very occupied with my responsibilities at the church, which, thankfully, remained only a twenty minute walk down the hill from our home. Sundays were ministry days, filled to the brim. Occasionally we would attend the big church but more often than not Bobbi and I would stop there only long enough to greet friends before continuing on to a slum area at the old railways. The train I had traveled on with my father as a young boy was no longer running, however, its abandoned tracks had quickly transformed into a bustling community. It consisted of an immense maze of makeshift shacks and shelters that housed many families.

The railway slum, which we referred to by its location, Abinchi, overflowed with both young and old all in desperate need. In addition to extreme poverty there is an abundance of addiction in this place. It was not uncommon to meet men, youth, and some women as well, intoxicated at all hours of the day. They would sit with their brimming calabashes (traditional bowls made from the halves of dry gourds) drinking strong liquor outside dirt floored shanty bars. To this place we went each week bringing the joy of Jesus' love and hope of His kingdom. Upon arrival we immediately were surrounded by our friends. Amid hugs and handshakes, dancing feet and shouts of welcome, we joined in the laughter and joyful noise as the entourage of boisterous youngsters grew around us.

Sometimes we were able to share food together but always on Sunday mornings the kids gathered to hear bible stories, eat peanuts, pray and sing songs with us. Some wore colorful dresses with soiled, lace bows and snagged ribbons, while others wore hardly a rag. Together we often walked around the community praying for individuals and visiting families, loving the ones we met. Our ministry team ranged from little toddlers clinging to our hands as their tiny bare feet wobbled along, to the young teenagers bounding ahead. Our good friend Kofi was such a faithful assistant to the children's ministry in Abinchi and to this day he continues to share Jesus there.

We would arrive back to the city church usually as their service was just letting out. Well dressed church members often eyed us up and down with a certain curious dismay, but this did not dampen our spirits. After all, a morning in Abinchi always left us covered in dirt and soot, and it was no unusual thing to find ourselves quite sticky also from all the tiny tears or runny noses we'd come into contact with, not to mention our own sweat. The smells of smoldering smoked fish clung to our clothes, and occasionally we became the substitute diaper in exchange for hugging the smallest of friends. It certainly wasn't a look that fit in with the fancy church look but we weren't phased by the occasional glances of alarm. Every ounce of dirt we carried home was well worth the joy of bringing Jesus to "The least of these." Matthew 25:40

**Tiniest house with the longest hallway**

While a mansion in comparison to what was found in Abinchi, our house was small enough that it did not come with an inside bathroom, laundry or kitchen. Thankfully, my previous room at the church transformed quite nicely into a kitchen for us. We did not have running water in our makeshift kitchen so we'd carry buckets from the well outside and lug the clean water upstairs. After using it we would then lug the dirty dishwater back downstairs to the gutter below.

Every day we walked to our kitchen at the church to cook one hot meal in the afternoon. Often on the way to our kitchen, we used to laugh together that our tiny house was a mansion because it took us twenty minutes to walk from our living room to our kitchen.

The church was also a place to call home for a number of single young men. So it came as no surprise for us to find our table often invaded at mealtime with lots of hungry brothers. A meal for two could easily become a meal for four, five, six or even eight adults. In my country when you are eating and a guest arrives at mealtime, we always try to be generous with our food. We tell them, "You are welcome." As it so happened with the smells of hot food floating

139

across the church grounds on such a consistent daily basis we began to have a lot of guests and "You are welcome" became our custom at most mealtimes.

On the other hand, there were the ants and mice, all of whom were not welcome guests. Almost overnight they decided to move in and set up their own operations alongside us in the kitchen. A rapid trip to the market found us armed with mouse bait, traps, bleach, and other disinfectant products to rid our kitchen of critters. The mice and ants continued to come in great numbers and no matter what we tried, it appeared to be a losing battle. One resolute afternoon I resorted to a glue trap. Stealthily, I placed the trap behind the stove. And then literally, in less than one hour, four mice had been caught in broad daylight. This shocking victory turned out to be quite distressing for my new wife Bobbi. While she hated the mice, she simply couldn't bear to see the fluffy things suffer this way. Away went our glue trap and out came the bleach. Every day thereafter Bobbi doused the surfaces of our kitchen before cooking.

**A good fight of faith**

"Wake up, honey!" I patted my wife's shoulder gently but firmly as she stirred in her sleep. "It's time to pray." Bobbi opened one sleepy eye to look at me, "What time is it?" she asked drowsily. When I told her it was midnight she slowly opened the other eye, "Okay." she replied and began to get up. The night before we had decided to pray together at the very start of the coming day. In my mind the start of the day would be just that, right now. Praying during the night hours was my preference, the quiet of night was undisturbed and invigorating. My wife on the other hand likes to sleep at night and pray first thing in the morning. Together we make for a very good prayer team. But on this particular night it was the two of us up at midnight.

There were a lot of hurdles that needed to be overcome in the course of our immigration journey to the United States. God's blessing had been profoundly evident throughout the long process, but in many ways it had not been an easy course to navigate. I had already been denied at the embassy on two prior interviews with no explanation given at the time of denial. This was becoming an expensive and frustrating process. The fees for each appointment quickly added up and yet both costly visits were so short and cut off so abruptly that I couldn't help wondering if they had even heard me say my name through the glass window. The up and coming interview for our marriage visa was precariously critical. More than anything else we were seeking the Lord's hand to cover us and our journey forward.

That night as we turned our attention to prayer we found ourselves facing a fight of faith such as we had never experienced as a couple. Before we could even begin praying one word or sing one song, Bobbi cried out in pain and doubled over on the cement floor. She couldn't walk and kept crying about a terrible pain inside of her. It had started instantly and was very aggressive. Due to a late service the night before we had decided to remain that night in our church kitchen, which contained a small room off to the side providing a simple place to relax. I picked Bobbi up in my arms and walked quickly across the dark grounds to the church building. Inside the quiet sanctuary I carried her to the front of the church and laid her there on a row of chairs, all the while she struggled in pain barely able to do more than cry. As I prayed I pulled the bottle of olive oil from the pulpit and anointed my suffering wife. And that is exactly when, as instantly as it had started, the pain left her. Bobbi sat up and told me "The pain is completely gone!". She stood up and walked around with no hesitation or pain. We thanked the Lord with such grateful hearts and proceeded to have a powerful time of prayer together interceding for all that was ahead of us.

This was clearly a direct demonic attack; however, instead of causing our faith and prayers to diminish this occurrence resulted in more devotion to prayer and praise than ever. What the devil meant for evil God had used for good.

**Goodness of God**

The look on my wife's face was hard to resist, especially as it combined with the luscious pile of fresh green coconuts before us. It was another day in the market for groceries and as often happened on market days, a treat of fresh coconuts usually became our indulgence. "Shall we then?" She asked, eyeing the fruit eagerly. "Of course!" I agreed with a smile. Reaching into my pocket I pulled out the small change needed for the priceless delicious nuts. In no time at all the coconut seller had swung his machete, skillfully removing the outside shell. With one final crack the top was off without even a drop of juice falling to the ground. The skill involved in preparing this knife wielding treat never ceased to amaze us. Bobbi picked out a pink straw from the selection offered to her and carefully accepted the coconut in both hands. Soon we were both enjoying a sweet ending to our successful market trip.

We walked home that day loaded with provision. Upon arriving at the house I gratefully unloaded the bags and with laughter said, "Bobbi do you realize just how I am blessed? Not only do I get to be your husband but I also get to be your security officer, your bargain finder and bartering man, your shopping cart in the market and your wheelbarrow to bring it all home!" she leaned over and kissed me, "Well then, I am a very blessed woman!" She laughed along with me before continuing, "Now, please leave the clean up to me and go take it easy for a while."

I walked outside and sat down to relax under the mango tree. It truly was a beautiful day, one of those kinds that would do well to last long into our forever memories. The final rays of sunshine filtered through the leaves of the mango tree above, scattering orange glows of light like a blanket around my feet. I let out a sigh of contentment. *God, You have been so good to me.*

Suddenly a loud cackle sounded from the avocado tree in the yard. I looked across in time to see a large crow jump from his perch and soar into the evening air. Seeing the common bird, my thoughts carried me back to the time when my brother Charles and I had to stand up for our faith to our old senior pastor. Once again, I was overwhelmed with the thought, *God you were right there too in that crazy time of shaking! You knew the plans You had for me.*

The landscape around where I sat was full of memories. To my left, standing as strong as ever even while the paint had long since given way to rust, was the front gate where I had entered for the first time as a cautious youth. The tent church had been pitched right there inside to welcome me. Out beyond the front gate lay the road leading to the roundabout which circled back towards my childhood village. Dakojum, the old village where the devil had tried to claim me as his baby, where my own blood had linked me to the side of evil. I smiled to recall how that very same place was right where the love of Jesus hit me with a rock on my head. What a strangely effective way God had used to catch my attention and reveal to me the significance of the blood of His own life shed to make me whole. *God You were right beside me when I didn't even know who You were. You knew the plans You had for me.*

Behind where I sat was the open space of grass where once a rusty red container had been the place where my six friends and I had called home for eight years. There to the right of me was the bathhouse. I was reminded of the day I went in there to hide my tears as I cried out to God for hope when the future looked so bleak and unknown. *God, I didn't feel it then but You were right there with me in that moment and You knew the plans You had for me.*

I smiled again to think of how God had brought me back to this place, not alone, but with my precious wife. We were to be here for a season of which God alone knew the length, but what a beautiful season it was. Glancing to the sky I thought about the days ahead when we would leave Ghana. To be honest, the road ahead of Bobbi and I was full of a multitude of unknowns. Marriage was new to us and family was merely a dream in our hearts. One day soon I would live in a new land, having a new place to call home. A foreign culture and people would be mine to embrace. Yes, the road ahead was certainly full of unrevealed things, but I knew it would also be full of opportunities to trust God. And I solidly, confidently knew as I thought back, that the faithfulness of God that had carried me throughout those now many years and brought me here today, would also take care of all tomorrow's unknowns. *I don't have a clue what to expect God but I do know You will be right there no matter what. Your plans are my hope.*

The goodness of God continued to overwhelm me as many more memories of His faithfulness filled me up that day. Tears of gratitude slipped freely down from my eyes as the timeless words of David, prayed so long ago, became my prayer of gratitude as well.

"Who am I, O Lord God, and what is my house that You have brought me this far?" 1 Chronicles 17:16

# Chapter 15 - Bobbi's Memories

"Delight yourself also in the Lord,
and He will give you the desires of your heart.
Commit your way to the Lord,
Trust also in Him, and He will bring it to pass."
~ Psalm 37:4-5 ~

A fter meeting Michael for the first time on the Africa Mercy Ship at lunch that day, I quickly lost sight of him amid all the busy preparations for our upcoming voyage. It wasn't until a week later, the day before we set sail for Sierra Leone actually, that our paths crossed again. During dinner an older gentleman stood up in the dining room to tell us about a prayer meeting in the ship's International lounge. It was scheduled for seven o'clock that very evening. I decided to go and yet when I opened the door to the large meeting room I stopped short, other than this older gentleman sitting near the front, the room was visibly empty. *How can no one else be here? I'll just leave quietly,* I reasoned to myself. Having not been seen, I quietly turned around and proceeded to walk away. And that is right when Holy Spirit nudged me to reconsider. He reminded me of the scripture, "Where two or three are gathered in My Name, there I am in the midst of them" Matthew 18:20 "You'd make two Bobbi and after all, prayer is important." Awkward or not, I knew what I needed to do, so turning around I went back inside. I was grateful to see a couple of others show up momentarily after I arrived and soon the prayer meeting was underway.

As we prayed that evening another person entered the room and sat down behind me. As this person prayed something so special took place that to this day I don't fully know how to describe it, other than to say, it was one of those incredible God moments that imprint themselves on our hearts. I tried to hold them in, but quickly tears started finding their way out of my tightly shut eyes, the presence of God was heavy in the room. There was something so precious with this prayer, unlike anything I had ever heard before. The person was so passionate speaking to God just as if he were talking to his own beloved father.

As soon as the prayer meeting came to a close, I turned around as quickly as was polite to do so in order to see who it was who had been praying so passionately behind me. To my surprise that's when I recognized Michael from lunch the previous week. Instantly I recalled the words, "Prayer." that he gave me in response to a question I'd asked him of how he came to the ship. Initially I was confused by what he meant, but now I found myself fascinated and I wanted to find out more about him. I was captivated and intrigued by the relationship he had with God, this was what my own heart longed for. Unfortunately, before I gathered courage to even say one word Michael had left the room, seemingly oblivious to the impact he had just made.

Neither of us recall exactly how we met up after this time, other than to know that we simply became friends. Amid the busy ship life, we found time on occasions to talk and pray together. Deep down inside I began to treasure more than I could put words to this incredible man of God.

Michael's life was a continuous picture of devotion to Jesus and love towards people. His soft and serious heart at times caused his eyes to spill over in tears when he saw or talked about the pain of people who were hurting. Michael's closeness to God was a constant inspiration to me. All in all he was a happy guy and a fun loving friend to everyone, especially the children who would always capture his heart.

One day shortly before I was to leave the ship and return to California, Michael asked if he could talk with me. He invited me to join him at a table in the place we called mid-ship and I happily obliged. Soon I was seated and eager to hear what he might have to say. First he began to tell me of how God had placed a passion into his heart for missions. I smiled and nodded as my friend talked about this and other things relating to his life calling. All was going well when the conversation suddenly took an abrupt turn, "Bobbi, I need to tell it to you like this. If I were wearing a shirt with a pocket in the front, there's something you have to understand about my pocket." I leaned in to understand, not wanting to miss even one word. Michael continued, "I have room in my pocket for God, I have room in my pocket for Jesus and I have room in my pocket for Holy Spirit. But, I do not have room in my pocket for you." That was it. The message he wanted to share had been delivered. *What!?* I sat there in silent shock wondering how on earth to respond. I certainly knew I had never ever asked to be in Michael's pocket, in fact, up to this point there was nothing romantic about our friendship at all, we hadn't even so much as shook hands in greeting.

Now honestly, yes, I was becoming increasingly fond of Michael, but I would not even allow myself to imagine anything more than him being a good friend. Had God revealed to him these innermost thoughts that I wasn't even willing to fully admit to myself? Sitting there at the table I tried hard not to show any outward shock. Although I honestly have to admit that inwardly my jaw dropped open and I sat stunned by his left field statement. Smiling as nonchalantly as I could I agreed with my friend that God had a perfect plan for his life.

The chances of us even remaining friends after I left the ship were slim. In the following days I couldn't stop wondering why Michael would say something like this so out of the blue, and yet so boldly blatant. My only supposition was that it was he, not I, who was struggling with his own feelings over our friendship. I was shocked at the curtness and saddened at the sudden ending to any hope that may or may not have been starting to rise in me. But I couldn't be upset with Michael and we remained great friends. We prayed together the morning I was to start my journey home to California. This last day on the ship was the first time we held hands and prayed. It was a precious moment. I knew I would never forget this friend however far life removed us. Michael left quickly after the prayer without so much as a parting wave, he was needed on the deck and I had to pack. However, he said he'd come to say goodbye when I left for the airport later that day. When the time arrived to leave, I scanned those railings of the ship and earnestly looked towards the gangway for one last encounter with Michael, but sadly he was nowhere to be seen. We never did say goodbye that day.

Upon returning home to California, I told my family about Michael. My mum asked me, "Bobbi, who knows maybe Michael is the one for you?" I laughed aloud and sighed, "Oh Mum, that is impossible! Not only are we from different countries and cultures but goodness, his Ghanaian accent is so strong I barely can understand what he's saying half the time." I couldn't bring myself to tell her that even Michael himself had vowed that there was no room in his pocket. We did however pray together that day over this friendship.

As the months went on occasionally I wrote to Michael, we even spoke on the phone a couple times but quickly our communication lessened. However, when Michael left the ship his communication stopped altogether. In fact for over the next nine months I heard nothing from Michael, I had little knowledge of what was going on in his life other than to see an occasional post on his public blog page. I knew he was working with God as a missionary, I was proud of him and yet missed him deeply. This was strange because we had been friends for a mere three months on the ship, however, I simply could not forget him. His silence was a sad and confusing reality. At one point I felt burdened to transfer a certain amount of money to Michael. I had no idea what he was doing let alone how much of a serious predicament he was facing in Uganda. I cared for Michael, my distant and silent friend. His picture had found a place in my bible and I prayed for him often. Although there was no room in his pocket for me there was room in my bible for him. I told myself that even if I never were to get married it would be okay for I knew that somewhere out there was an incredible man of God that I could have so easily fallen in love with.

Strangely right before flying to Africa for a second time, I received a short message from Michael. It came clear out of the blue and I was stunned. The message was short but thoughtful. And yet, Michael was still such a far away mystery in so many ways. It is hard to continually miss someone with absolutely no hope of ever seeing them again on this planet. Finally my emotions poured themselves out as I was sitting on a bench in the hot sun of Mozambique. I was so over not being able to let go of the memory of Michael especially when clearly he had moved on. I cried out to God in prayer, "Please Father, please take away this longing in my spirit for Michael. I bless his life, and his passion for You Lord. But Father God I just don't want to think about Michael anymore. He has moved on and I desperately want to be able to move on too." I sat there with tears on my face, looking up towards heaven. The only thing I heard was a still small voice whisper, "Bobbi, I want you to trust Me." I knew God was speaking to my heart, His words were so soft and confident. I continued to cry for I couldn't understand anything about all this. I chose to surrender to my Heavenly Father. I didn't know what He had for me in the future but one day the hope filled plans He had for my life would be revealed, even if the current circumstance was painful to endure.

In God's perfect timing He brought Michael and I back into a strong friendship which grew quickly. Like only He could do God put me squarely in Michael's pocket, which miraculously had grown big enough to accommodate me. We were soon married. The two year interim had challenged and grown both of our spiritual journeys and when we did reconnect we found ourselves closer than ever could have been possible at the start of our friendship. When that perfect time came for us to be together forever, it was the happiest moment of our lives. On the day of our wedding we were both undone by God's gracious hand as now we could look back and see how skillfully the Lord had woven together our vastly different stories into a beautiful tapestry of love.

I was 28 years old when I married Michael and he was 33. At times it had felt like single cold storage but I refused to be desperate to find a husband. God's love stories are always the best. When I thought of what a marriage could look like for me or how it would come about, I could never have dreamed the story He was about to write.

"Jesus looked at them and said, with man this is impossible but not with God for with God all things are possible." Matthew 19.26

# Author Contact and Ministry Resources

Michael Bentum

P.O. Box 353
Upper Lake, CA 95485

Made in USA - North Chelmsford, MA
1321785_9780578384627
07.13.2022 1011